UNSTOPPABLE

SCRIBE: BRAD KAUFFMAN, BRAD.
KAUFFMAN@SCRIBEMEDIA.COM AND SUSAN
PAUL, SUSAN.PAUL@SCRIBEMEDIA.COM

PUBLISHERS: JOHN VERCHER, JOHN.
VERCHER@SCRIBEMEDIA.COM AND JAMES
TIMBERLAKE, JAMES.TIMBERLAKE@
SCRIBEMEDIA.COM

LIONCREST
PUBLISHING

To You, the reader. Everything is going to be okay. If you're going through hell, keep going, and use this book as your roadmap to see your way through. You got this.

And to Bally: Thank you for getting me through this. You were just what I needed.

CONTENTS

BEFORE WE BEGIN

If you think you're having a heart attack, please get to the hospital. If you're having an anxiety or panic attack, please go to your doctor. Everything's eventually going to be okay, but you first need to address any serious health concerns before you read this book.

On the topic of medical advice, I'm not a doctor. I don't play one on TV (or even on the Internet). I simply know what has worked for me and my fellow entrepreneurs for managing and overcoming the anxiety that comes with starting and running a rapidly growing business.

I also never used any prescription, over-the-counter, or recreational medications to beat my crippling anxiety attacks and do not discuss them in this book. Though I took an all-natural approach, your doctor's advice comes first; the methods in this book are secondary.

That said, the bottom line is that if you're an overwhelmed, stressed-out business owner struggling with anxiety, you're in the right place. The strategies in this book will help you get through this hell and leave you Unstoppable. They'll show you how to beat stress and dominate in business and life. And even if you don't suffer from full-blown anxiety attacks, this book will still give you more clarity and focus, stop you from feeling overwhelmed, and make you happier, healthier, and more successful.

THE POINT OF NO RETURN

On New Year's Day in 2006, I woke up at the tail end of a three-day bender. Hungover and exhausted, I crawled out of bed around noon, stumbled to the bathroom, and took a shower, hoping it would ease my pain.

That's when the real trouble started.

As I stood under the water, it became hard to catch my breath. My chest tightened. My heart started racing.

"Oh my God, I'm having a heart attack," I thought.

Up until that point in my life, I was indestructible: a hard-charging, thirty-year-old, know-it-all entrepreneur. "Nothing can stop me," I would brag to my friends after another twelve-hour workday and six-drink minimum at the bar.

Even as I stood there in the shower with that crushing sensation in my chest, part of me shrugged it off and I thought—just like my throbbing headache—that it was temporary, like all my other hangovers in the past. There was no cause for alarm. I just needed a nap and some Gatorade, and everything would get back to normal in time for Monday morning.

Except it didn't.

Instead, things got worse. Lying down made the beating of my heart stronger. Sitting made me realize how difficult it was to breathe. Ten minutes passed, then an hour. I couldn't sleep, eat, or concentrate. I spent the next several hours pacing back and forth across my tiny, downtown Toronto apartment, my feeling of invincibility giving way to fear and helplessness.

Somehow, I discovered that sitting down to pee offered short-term relief. For the next several hours, I would pace for twenty minutes, then stop to pee like a girl and get a brief break from the madness.

As I sat there, I visualized the worst-case scenario.

I'm going to die alone in my apartment, a pathetic, thirty-year-old loser. No one will even notice I'm missing for days. Ugh, and my mom's going to be really embarrassed trying to explain this at church next week.

I was terrified by the thought of a one-line Wikipedia page about my life that read, "Craig had so much potential, and he spent all his time in the gym and at bars chasing girls. The rest of it he wasted.."

That sad biography would overshadow the fact that I had worked myself into the ground for the past year building my business. The chronic stress, combined with physical exhaustion from drinking too much and not sleeping enough, had led me to this pivotal moment in my life.

I thought about the decisions that had brought me to this point: I was burning the candle at both ends. By day I was working all hours without any boundaries. Several nights a week, I was out until 3 a.m. Being able to do whatever I wanted whenever I wanted didn't just catch up with me—it nearly broke me.

Finally, after hours of pacing, peeing, and fearing the worst, I gave up. At 11 p.m. I tapped out and decided to go to the emergency room. This was my point of no return.

I walked down the eight flights of stairs in my apartment building (to avoid the awkwardness of dying in an elevator with strangers) and headed outside. It was a Sunday night, New Year's Day, and the cold, snowy streets of Toronto were empty and depressing, but somehow, I immediately began to feel better in the fresh air. I waved down the first cab that went by.

Lesson #1: When anxiety attacks, get outside. Staying inside only makes it worse.

"Can you take me to the hospital, please?" I asked the driver. Just saying those few words to a total stranger eased my anxiety even further.

Lesson #2: When anxiety attacks, get out of your own head. Talk to someone. Let them know you need help. Bottling up your thoughts and letting your wheels spin only makes your anxiety worse.

The cabbie dropped me off in front of the emergency room of Toronto General Hospital. Lucky for me, the ER was empty. As I walked in, the receptionist, a young man around my age, looked up from his paperwork and stared at me with a mixture of surprise and contempt as if to say, "What do *you* want, buddy?"

"I think I'm having a heart attack," I said.

Instantly, his demeanor changed. His jaw dropped, as if I had guessed some password that let me into a secret society where the doctors and nurses gave you immediate attention.

"Come back here," he said, escorting me to a stretcher. I lied down, and a nurse appeared. The next half-hour was a haze of tests and interrogation punctuated with awe at my New Year's debauchery.

"You drank HOW MANY Red Bulls last night?" she asked.

"Seven," I repeated.

She looked at me in disbelief. After mentally filing that away for another "crazy story from the ER" to tell her friends, she took my blood pressure, measured my heart rate, and placed her hand on mine. As soon as she did that simple act of human touch gave me the sense of peace I'd been searching for all day.

Lesson #3: When anxiety attacks, get connected. Human touch and conversation can go a long way in easing your fears and calming you down.

Between her touch and the doctor's diagnosis that I was not, in fact, having a heart attack, my anxiety seemed to almost disappear in mere minutes.

I was in and out of the emergency room in less an hour. My recovery had happened so swiftly and with no specific treatment that the incident felt like a dream. Had I imagined it? Or had I really spent an entire day alone in my condo, convinced I was about to die?

After getting quick relief from my first full-blown attack, I decided to turn over a new leaf. I went to a couple of yoga sessions. I gave meditation a half-hearted try. I didn't drink that weekend. But having been freed from the anxiety, my old lifestyle—the long days and longer nights—soon started to creep back in. Two weeks later, I returned to my old ways: too much caffeine, working too many hours, drinking too much alcohol—and staying up until my normal weekday wake-up time on Saturday night.

Pretending I was fine was more convenient than dealing with the truth.

Of course, I was not fine, and my quick recovery in the emergency room gave me a false sense of security. By complete accident, I'd stumbled upon some effective remedies for dealing with anxiety: a walk outside in the fresh air, the comfort of human conversation, and the calming reassurance of human touch.

Though I didn't realize it at the time, New Year's Day 2006 marked a new chapter in my life and the first fight in a long battle with anxiety.

Looking back, I'd had previous brushes with anxiety in college and during my mid-twenties. More than once, I'd been in extremely stressful situations and found myself unable to breathe deeply. I remember pacing outside the office at my first real job with tightness in my chest, desperately trying to catch my breath. These were warning shots that I chose to ignore.

Like many entrepreneurs, I'm what you would call a Type-A person, demanding, always impatient and rushing. I held myself and others to unreasonable expectations. I could never be successful enough, projects could never be done fast enough, and my identity and self-worth relied heavily on monetary success. And when I couldn't find fulfillment at work, I went looking for it at the bar.

But now, I'd suffered a real anxiety attack and when that happens, you can't put the genie back in the bottle. You can try to ignore it, repress it, and hide under a cloak of invincibility, but anxiety attacks are like cockroaches. If you've got one, there are a lot more hiding in your attic.

The Anxiety Strikes Back

Three months later, back to my old ways—and more—I had an epic night out. It started with day-drinking in a pub, moved to a club, and ended with an after-party. I left a girl's house at six in the morning, threw up on her lawn, and grabbed a cab home. (Yes, I was *that guy*.)

I slept until four in the afternoon, grabbed some fast food with a friend where I tried to piece together the previous night, and then went home and went right back to bed. Add another tale to the long list of frat-boy adventures of Craig Ballantyne.

But this wasn't just another hangover that I could sleep off. That night, I had a strange, dark dream, and I woke up the next morning with an unshakeable sense of impending doom.

Thirty minutes after I woke up, the fire alarm went off in my condo building. I walked outside, sat on a park bench, and stared at the sunny skies. It was the perfect spring day, but my anxiety was mounting a comeback.

"You'll be fine. It'll go away like last time," I thought. After all, I was invincible. Nothing could hold me down.

Wrong again.

That morning was the start of my six-week "heart attack." Twenty-four hours a day, seven days a week, for the next month-and-a-half, I had the same symptoms I'd experienced on New Year's Day. There was the tight chest, the struggle to breathe, the elevated heart rate, and the tingling from the top of my head to the end of my fingertips.

Rather than head back to the emergency room or seek medical help of any kind, I stubbornly tried to fix the problem myself. "I've dealt with this before," I thought, "and I'll deal with it again."

The Experiments Begin

After several days, I reluctantly asked one of my friends for help. He suggested qigong, which is a standing meditation technique similar to tai chi. "Worth a try," I thought. "That one yoga session I tried in January seemed to help, so I'm sure that if I do this once or twice, I'll be cured."

As it turned out, the qigong instructor lived in a tiny apartment in a massive building that looked like it belonged in Soviet Russia, not the middle of Toronto. The apartment smelled like cigarettes (*Seriously? A meditation teacher that smoked cigarettes?*). And the instructor was even more socially awkward than me, a real serial-killer type. Despite worrying that I had a good chance of ending up chopped up in this guy's freezer, I managed to attend weekly sessions for a month. In my desperation, I also gave yoga, tai chi, and meditation another shot. But I hated all of them and wasn't convinced they were making any difference.

I was wrong. Again. (Seeing a trend here?) Even though I eventually gave up on qigong and the other classes, these techniques delivered a big breakthrough. They taught me to breathe properly. Here I was, thirty years old, with three decades of experience in the art of breathing... and yet, I'd been doing all wrong. Today, the lesson I learned in those classes is one of my strongest weapons in keeping my anxiety away. I just couldn't see that back then.

Lesson #4: When anxiety attacks, breathe. Done properly, breathing can have an immediate calming effect on your body and your mind.

I learned these lessons the hard way so that you don't have to. Today, they are invaluable tools that keep me anxiety free through even the busiest, most stressful times (like hitting book deadlines). Though I wouldn't want to repeat the experiences I went through to learn them, it was worth it in the long run to uncover these secrets that allowed me to conquer my anxiety for good – and so that you can too.

Anxiety is a funny thing. The more you focus on fixing it, the worse it seems to get. And even if you manage to shake it off temporarily, just when you think you're getting better, something—such as a random conversation with a friend or a seemingly innocuous incident at work—can trigger that panic in your mind and body again.

Anxiety also consumes your thoughts. You can't focus. You're easily overwhelmed. At best, you operate at 60 percent of your capacity. Trapped in a physical and mental prison, your instinct is to find an escape—any escape. But drinking makes it worse (eventually) and even sleep provides little sanctuary. During my six-week heart attack, I'd be lucky to pass out at eleven at night (after lying there for an hour) before my anxiety woke me up like a drill sergeant from hell at three in the morning.

Even my healthy habits of diet and exercise were thrown off track. I tried to stick to my regular workouts, but the thought of increasing my already elevated heart rate sent my mind into a hypochondriatic tailspin. The irony of me, a fitness expert, dying while doing his own workouts crossed my mind many times.

Anxiety also messes with and suppresses your appetite. I was so worried about losing my hard-earned muscle mass that I resorted to eating junk food, so I wouldn't waste away to nothing. Of course, you don't have to be a nutrition expert to know the excess sugar contributed to the vicious cycle of stress and anxiety that becomes so hard to escape.

Unable to sleep or eat, I plunged deeper into my own personal hell. I'd wander the streets of Toronto hoping for relief from a "hit" of fresh air. One morning on my way back from a long 4 a.m. walk, I grabbed a chocolate bar. I got into my building's elevator with a guy returning from his morning run.

"Breakfast of champions," the jogger said, looking at the candy bar in my hand.

So I punched him in the face, curing my anxiety forever. The end.

If only it were that simple. The truth was, his comment made me more self-conscious and anxious, just like so many other moments can when I kept things bottled up, let my mind race, and avoided those lessons I had learned before.

The Triggers in Your Head

When you deal with anxiety, there will be days when you think everything is going to be fine. "Awesome, I'm back to normal!" you'll think on a good morning, and like me, you'll be tempted to shrug off everything you've been through and go back to your old behaviors. That's precisely when a trigger will come along and turn your life upside down.

With anxiety, the smallest, random day-to-day interactions can set you off into a vicious cycle of mental self-destruction. Your worst thoughts spin out of control in your head. The only way out is to break the cycle, but when anxiety is new, you don't know what helps and what hurts.

Halfway through my six-week heart attack, I began to feel like myself again. I even felt well enough to go to the gym and do a hard training session.

Near the end of my workout, I saw an old friend from college. "Great," I thought, "Say a quick 'hello,' don't let him see what you're going through, and get back to your bench pressing." Of course, that quick hello turned into a five-minute conversation. Just as we were finishing up, he said, "You know, life's crazy. Just the other day a guy I know who's about our age had a stroke from too much partying."

Cue the anxiety engine. My mind started racing again and neurotic brain kicked into overdrive. "Is that what's going to happen to me next?" I thought, "Is that how *I'm* going to go down?"

It's funny (in hindsight, of course, because there was nothing funny about it at the time) how a seemingly harmless comment from a friend could trigger an anxiety response, setting in motion a destructive loop that played over and over in my head day after day for weeks at a time.

It reminded me of an old *Star Trek* movie, where the "bad guys" (sorry, I'm not a Trekkie) put these giant bugs inside the ears of the good guys, torturing them and driving them mad. That's how it feels when you have anxiety. One offhand comment can stir up a memory or emotion that you can't get out of your head. Your mental wheels begin to race, revving your anxiety engine, and you imagine the problem getting worse and worse, while any solution begins to appear more and more impossible. Your fears expand, and the situation seems hopeless. Your anxiety feeds on your worries and grows, eventually paralyzing you because it's all you can think about.

My friend's comment at the gym extended my anxiety for weeks. Heck, it's been over a decade since that day, and the conversation still makes me cringe. "You're next," my anxiety brain worm said. "You're next."

During those six weeks, I turned over every rock I could, searching for a solution but finding no relief. Desperate for help, I did what any normal person would do when they needed medical attention. I bought a dog.

Paging Dr. Bally

For several months, I had been thinking about getting a dog for all the normal reasons (like meeting girls). Now I had another motive. During my deep dive into fixing my mental health, I had read that petting a dog reduces symptoms of depression and anxiety.

"A-ha," I thought. "All I need is a puppy. That'll be the answer to all my problems." (*Insert sarcastic eyeroll.*)

A friend recommended a breeder just north of the city. When I called on a Friday, they had two puppies left in the latest litter, so I drove out on Saturday morning. As I was debating which one to choose, a little brown furball puppy-bounded over and peed right beside my leg, marking his spot.

"Well, I guess that's the one," I said. We went inside to sign some forms, making my dog ownership—and his name, Bally—official. Then I put Bally in the back of my car and off we went back to the big city.

The poor little guy cried all the way home, which was, of course, another source of anxiety for me. "Don't worry, bud," I said to him, "When we get home, I'll take you for a big walk!" That's what dogs love to do, right? And getting outside would relieve my anxiety, too. Finally, I'd found the secret ingredient to a successful recovery.

Wrong.

We got home, I set up his crate inside, and we went out for our walk. Correction: I dragged him outside. Stubborn little Bally parked himself on the floor of my apartment's lobby and didn't want to go anywhere. He hated being on a leash (and always did). Eventually, I got him across the street to a park, but he sat down there, too. I begged him to walk. I bribed him with treats. I tried pushing him. I tried pulling him. Nothing seemed to work. Worried that someone was going to call the Humane Society on me, I gave up and carried him back inside.

The next day, Bally and I drove over to a park where we could play fetch. He was a Labrador Retriever, after all. Key word, "retriever." That's what they do, right? Retrieve things?

"Alright buddy," I said, letting him off his leash. I pulled out an old tennis ball and threw it. "Go get it!"

No dice.

I walked over, fetched the ball, and put it in front of his nose in hopes of signaling to him that the game was on. I threw it again—this time not so far.

Bally took this as a signal to lie down.

I tried again and again, but he clearly had no interest in playing fetch, and he never would. (The only thing Bally ever fetched was a treat.)

On Monday, his third day in the big city, I left Bally at home while I attended some business meetings. When I returned a few hours later, my apartment door was covered with nasty notes threatening to have us kicked out.

The poor little guy had been crying all morning because he had a severe case of separation anxiety. Left alone, he was frightened, worried, overwhelmed, and confused.

Then I realized: I had bought the dog version of me!

Over the next three weeks, having Bally around actually made my anxiety worse. The sleepless nights, the stubborn walks, the constant worry of him crying every time I left the apartment for five minutes, all of this external tension added to my internal stress. Of course, eventually, things got better, and he became one of the greatest joys in my life. But most importantly, just as the research had promised, the presence of Bally and his unconditional love became one of my best weapons in winning the war against anxiety.

There's Nothing Wrong with You

Exactly six weeks to the day after my anxiety had flared back up, I went to the gym to meet Richard, one of the few remaining clients from my personal training business.

It was another beautiful, sunny Monday morning—a perfect day (for normal people). Richard was a fifty-three-year-old, obese and overworked lawyer. He ate poorly, didn't sleep well, and was constantly stressed out. But he was a strong and kind-hearted man, and I always looked forward to our sessions. That morning, in a corner of the small boutique gym where we trained, I had Richard doing pushups when my anxiety reared its ugly head. I had been fighting it all morning, and perhaps it was that sense of literally having my back to the wall in that tiny studio that made the feeling *unbearable*.

Just like on New Year's Day, I had come to a point where I simply couldn't take it anymore.

Unfortunately, anxiety is like a Black Box. You can't explain it to yourself, and worse, you can't explain it to others. My feelings were all too real to me, but I couldn't show them to anyone else. It's not like having a broken arm, something that everyone can understand. Instead, anxiety is a crippling, unseen attack on your mind. It doesn't show up with visible symptoms, nor is it something that anyone who doesn't have anxiety can understand. This leaves you in a Catch-22 position, where your anxiety can grow worse because you can't properly describe it to others. That's what happened to me that morning, and why it became the moment that finally broke me.

"Richard," I said after his last pushup, "I need to go to the emergency room."

Richard was confused. He looked at me as if I had two heads. After all, if a stranger were to look at the two of us and seen a young, fit personal trainer standing beside his out-of-breath, sweaty, obese middle-aged client and had to choose which one needed to be going to the hospital that day, they would have picked Richard, not me. But after taking a moment to process this strange request, Richard kindly drove me to St. Michael's Hospital in downtown Toronto. The ride was short but awkward, and our relationship was never the same after that. My anxiety attack had shell-shocked us both.

St. Michael's is located at a gritty intersection on the edge of Toronto's financial district. It sits beside a church courtyard where people from all walks of life gather to play chess, and where homeless people set up camp and sleep. The sidewalks were full of office workers and girls in summer dresses walking to their jobs in nearby skyscrapers, while addicts from a local rehab clinic begged for change. The juxtaposition of these people on the streets matched the one between my physically healthy body and the chaos in my mind.

I walked into the ER and led with the same opener as I had in my New Year's Day routine, "I think I'm having a heart attack."

But this time my line fell flat. St. Michael's is one of Toronto's major trauma hospitals, and it's also located close to many rehab centers. Nothing I could say alarmed the experienced staff. They'd heard it all before, and besides, the emergency room was already packed.

"Take a seat," the receptionist said without making eye contact. "We'll call you when we're ready."

Two hours passed before getting into an examination room. Then I waited another half an hour until a nurse came to check my vital signs. The longer I waited, the more that guilt and shame replaced my anxiety, feeling that I was wasting the doctor's time and energy that could be better used on those other people out in the waiting area.

But I was wrong again. Anxiety is not something to dismiss or try to ignore. It's a real issue and I had finally made the right decision to take it seriously, and so must you.

Lesson #5: Get help.

Once again, just like on New Year's Day, the kind nurse assured me I wasn't having a heart attack. But this time, just to be sure there wasn't some underlying cause of my symptoms, the doctor ordered a chest x-ray. She also sent me home with a heart rate monitor to wear for the next twenty-four hours.

"When you return this tomorrow," she said, "We'll take a look at the data and contact you if there are any concerns. But if you don't hear from us within twenty-four hours, that means everything is fine."

As those twenty-four hours counted down, my anxiety slowly began to disappear.

While sitting at home, I continued seeking out solutions to my anxiety, and a Google search brought me to the website of an e-book called *Panic Away*. Buying it turned out to be one of the best decisions of my life – even though I never read past the first five words of Chapter Two.

It was there, in the very first sentence, that I found the *exact* words I needed to set me free. Simple, yet powerful, this line would "cure" me of my anxiety:

There's nothing wrong with you.

As soon as I read that sentence, it hit me: "There IS nothing wrong with me." The timing was perfect. The doctor's tests had proven it. These words had confirmed it. That was the moment that it felt like someone had unlocked a prison door and let me out.

And then I said something to myself that every entrepreneur, executive, and parent can relate to: "I'm too busy for this anxiety anyway." While I recognize the irony in being too busy for anxiety, you know what I mean. You and I both have so much going on, so many projects to tackle, so many people to help, and so much to do that we have no time to let anxiety attacks consume our lives.

Now while I felt cured of my anxiety on that day, I must admit that there were several times over the next two years where a trigger *almost* caused my anxiety to return. However, I had now learned five big lessons about overcoming anxiety andI had mastered several solutions to preventing panic attacks. These lessons, along with the knowledge that there was nothing physically wrong with me, always allowed me to fight it off and keep out of the prison that anxiety can bring. Whether it was making the decision to open up to a friend or taking time to do slow, deep belly breathing, I had built strong defenses, and even a strong offense to proactively attack anxiety. Today, despite my life being as busy and my business growing as fast as ever, my anxiety is under control thanks to the strategies revealed in this book.

And so, my friend, I promise that you, too, will find the keys to getting out—and staying out—of your anxiety prison in these pages too.

Today I live by this mantra, which you'll see me repeating in this book:

Action Beats Anxiety. Motion beats Meditation. Work Beats Worry.

Taking the first steps to solve your problem, even if they are small steps, is the right move in the right direction. It's always better than sitting and stewing about a problem or letting your anxiety build up.

Fortunately, you've picked up this book. You've made a very wise decision and taken a very important first step. This book, and the strategies within it, will lead you to the people and processes you need to beat anxiety and become Unstoppable again.

Ending Your Anxiety Forever

As an entrepreneur, you'll always have stress. The pressure is always going to be on, and the best things we can do are recognize it, prepare for it, and control it. When we are armed with the tools to fight off these feelings, we have what I call the "cure" for anxiety. That means having the simple strategies in place to prevent anxiety from ever wreaking havoc in your life again. While doctors might disagree on whether we can completely cure someone of anxiety, I know they'll agree that the methods in this book are some of the best ways to control it and allow you to become Unstoppable, so you can get back to dominating in business and in life.

Make no mistake about it, dealing with and suffering from anxiety is no joke. It can cripple your decision-making, and practically paralyze you when trying to live a normal life. Anxiety is also an increasingly common mental health issue—over *forty million people* are suffering from it, according to a June 2017 *New York Times* article.[1] But again, it can be overcome. I'm living proof and here to serve as your guide on your hero's journey as you do the same. This has become my mission in life, to help high performers like you overcome the terrible toll it can take.

There is a small (and very lucky) group of people who never experience anxiety. However, even if you're one of those anxiety-free people, you'll still benefit greatly from the strategies discussed in this book because they will bring you more clarity and focus, and you'll be ready to handle anxiety if it ever surfaces in your life—or the life of your loved ones.

But if you're like me and are prone to anxiety, this book will help you understand how to permanently liberate yourself from the black box of anxiety and its triggers. Reading this book will make you feel better and applying the strategies will help you become Unstoppable when your anxiety is finally all behind you.

Once you add these powerful anxiety-reducing habits, you won't need to worry about it dominating your life again. Sure, it might show up on your doorstep from time to time, but if it does, you'll be prepared to shut the door on it, and send it on its way.

That said, this is a journey, or what I'll be calling your "hero's journey." Freedom will come easier for some than others. But just as a simple line in a book changed my life for the better over a decade ago, the words in this book will also set you free.

Don't Feel Bad... They've Got It Too

While this book is for entrepreneurs, business owners, and executives who are dealing with anxiety, the problem exists for people in all walks of life. The number of Internet searches related to anxiety has nearly *doubled* in only five years, according to the previously cited *New York Times* article. Anxiety is an epidemic, and sadly, it's getting worse.

Crippling anxiety can even take down your favorite celebrity. In a 2011 *Rolling Stone* article, superstar vocalist Adele admitted to having frequent anxiety attacks before and during her shows. At one point she found herself vomiting before a show while sitting out on the fire escape of a major auditorium.[2] Some entertainers, like Chris Martin of Coldplay, have funny rituals and superstitions to get them past their anxiety. Even Bono, the lead singer of U2—despite twenty-five years of selling out stadiums—struggles with anxiety. "The morning before a show, I get nervous. I wake up with a sick feeling," he told *Harper's Bazaar*.[3]

Anxiety affects every type of person imaginable. Take my friend Larry W, for instance. Larry is a police officer in Texas and former Marine who spent three tours of duty in Iraq. As he made the transition back into civilian life, Larry began the process of opening a boot camp-style gym. Suddenly anxiety showed up in a major way, sending him to the emergency room at eleven o'clock on a Saturday night. Fortunately, Larry had heard me speak about my anxiety struggles at a fitness business summit, and so he messaged me from the emergency room for help – and I taught him what you'll learn in this book.

Larry's story shows us that anxiety can affect even the strongest of people. This is a man who was a *police officer*. A Marine who spent *six years in Iraq*. I get many messages from entrepreneurs like the one Larry sent me.

"Craig, I woke up at 2:00 a.m. with a crushing feeling in my chest and had to go to the doctor. Now I know what you were going through!"

"Craig, I'm overwhelmed. I'm starting to panic. What should I do?"

(And of course, I always refer people to their doctor or emergency room first. But once they've been discharged in good health, that's when the strategies in this book and my advice can help.)

Anxiety can bring *anyone* to their knees. It doesn't care how tough you are, anxiety spares no one: not cops, soldiers, athletes, musicians, mothers, teenagers, millennials, or senior citizens. A recent article in the *Telegraph* cited a spike in anxiety among women going through menopause. Then there's the "sandwich generation" of people who are taking care of their parents as well as their own children. Anxiety affects them too, along with millions of others. Anxiety doesn't care what you've done or how much you've got to do today; it's a risk and a reality for virtually *everybody*.

After more than a decade of coaching successful business owners and executives, I'm convinced that every one of them struggles with some form of High-Performance Anxiety. Sometimes it stems from our genetics, sometimes from long-lasting remnants of an abusive childhood, and sometimes, like it was for me, all of the above combined with poor lifestyle choices. Much of our anxiety, though, comes from the external world: society's pressures, comparison syndrome, the chase for more, and the never-ending demands for your time.

As business owners and high-performers, we don't show up for work and wait to be told what to do. We're responsible for our own schedules and our own incomes. If we have employees, we're responsible for the very livelihoods of dozens, hundreds, or even thousands of other people. There's a lot at stake and that leads to a lot of pressure, internal and external.

You are a very driven individual. You strive for ever-increasing success, want to do everything yourself, and worse—you believe that you can. You set extremely high standards for yourself and work hard to achieve your goals, but this drive combined with the pressures and responsibilities of running a business are also the perfect storm for anxiety. This is kind of ironic, since so many of us entrepreneurs are driven to be super-healthy and super-productive, yet the dedication to our businesses can produce the opposite results and a take a major toll on our lives.

Many high-performers are aware of the problem but do not prioritize it or believe they have time to deal with it. While we're extremely assertive, even aggressive, at tackling the non-stop issues we face in business, we often ignore the warning signs of anxiety and let it build up to a boiling point until it explodes into our lives.

Part of the problem is the uncertainty, unpredictability, and sense of the unknown around anxiety. The person suffering with anxiety struggles in silence, not knowing what exactly is happening or what to do about it. All they know for sure is they feel like they're having the worst day of their life and they don't know when that feeling will end.

Imagine an entrepreneur suffering through the worst day of her business. Sales are down, expenses are up, and while there's a glimmer of hope on the horizon about a big deal coming through, right now she's struggling to meet payroll and deadlines at work, all while contending with a busy family life at home. She's trying to hold it together, but it takes all her strength to avoid showing weakness to her employees, her vendors, and her competitors. Feelings of shame, embarrassment, and confusion pile on. Entrepreneurial Anxiety and the emotions it spawns can snowball into an overwhelming feeling of paralysis. With anxiety, you have no idea why your heart is racing, or why you can't make a decision. People can't understand why you don't want to go to the movies, or go to work, or meet up for dinner.

This is probably not how most people view the typical high-powered twenty-first century high performer, but it happens more often than you think.

What's the Deal With Anxiety?

To make matters worse, there's a stigma attached to mental health challenges when compared to physical problems. If someone is diagnosed with cancer, we get it. Born with Type-1 diabetes? Sorry to hear that.

But when you suffer from anxiety, ignorant people say things like, "Oh, it's all in your head. Shake it off. Quit complaining and get back to work." Your hard-charging business buddies razz you for needing a break. Cruel bosses roll their eyes at an employee for requesting help when they are overwhelmed.

The stigma surrounding mental health is part of the vicious cycle that makes anxiety worse and harder to overcome. When people feel ashamed and don't talk about their anxiety with those around them, it prevents them from seeking help, makes things worse, and keeps them locked in a prison of pain and panic, and that's *why* it was so important for me to write this book.

You know what? Forget those people. That's the first step you have to take on your hero's journey to getting better.

I'm going to tell you this now, and I'm going to repeat it several times throughout the book: *you're going to be okay.* If you've gone to the hospital and you are not having a heart attack, and your doctor has cleared you of any physical problems, then you are *not* going to drop dead from this anxiety. Everything's going to be alright.

Now I know what you're thinking. "That's easy for you to say."

And you're right. It is easy to say because I've gone through my hell and come out the other side stronger than ever, just as you will. Today, anxiety doesn't bother me, it doesn't hold me in a prison, and it doesn't cause me shame or embarrassment.

In fact, I've told, no, *bragged* about my anxiety story to millions of people in my books, speeches, and online in my YouTube videos. It doesn't bother me what people say because their words can never be as bad as the anxiety that I battled—and beat.

One day you'll feel like this, too. It's not that naïve feeling of invincibility that I had as a young man, but a feeling of wise assurance that I'm in control now.

It's my life's mission to make this message known. Over *forty million Americans* are going through this, and this number is growing. There are likely millions more who also suffer from anxiety and haven't yet identified it or sought help for it— simply because they can't understand what it is, or they are scared of being shamed for it.

You are *not* alone.

You *will* overcome this. You *will* be okay.

When you begin to believe this—truly *believe* it—you'll put yourself on the road to recovery, a road that I am committed to walk with you.

Join Me on Your Hero's Journey

On New Year's Day in 2006, I was a scared and confused young man trapped inside that terrifying black box of anxiety. The questions frantically flowed into my mind, causing me more anxiety.

Am I having a heart attack? Am I going crazy? Am I going to die?

During my six-week-long anxiety attack, scarier thoughts emerged. *Was I doomed to feel like this forever?* And while I never once considered suicide, I do remember thinking during one of my breaking points, "I would do anything to get rid of this feeling."

If those types of questions and feelings are going through your mind, it's okay.

Your first instinct will be to lock yourself in your room and hide. Please don't. Isolation is the *worst* thing you can do. When you go it alone, you're just going to spend more time inside your own head, with your wheels turning faster, your anxiety engine revving, and the pressure building up. Do *not* hold it in. Bottling it up is the last thing you want to do.

The first step is to talk to someone. You must get out of your own head.

Think about the main character in a horror movie, or if you prefer cartoons like I do, an episode of *Scooby-Doo*. Bad things start happening when characters break away from the group and go off on their own. Anxiety is no different. You are *not* going to overcome this by yourself. It's crucial for you to understand this point. Although it might feel difficult to open up to a friend about your anxiety, it's not nearly as difficult as trying to cure anxiety on your own.

While I made a lot of mistakes that put me in the path of anxiety, one of the wisest things I did was to set my ego aside and seek help. That led me to yoga, meditation, qigong, tai chi, proper breathing, asking for a ride to the hospital, going to the emergency room, getting clarity from a doctor, and reading the book, *Panic Away*. You must keep digging for answers, and it's best if you get others to help.

Action Beats Anxiety. Motion Beats Meditation. Work Beats Worry.

The Secret Ingredient: My Mentor

In every hero's journey, the protagonist has at least one wise sage to guide them on their way. Luke Skywalker had Obi-Wan and Yoda, Harry Potter had Dumbledore. I had Bally the Dog.

But I also had other mentors, real-life humans, who played an important role in helping me break free of anxiety.

The year 2006 was pivotal for me in more areas than just my health. Coincidently I started working with my first business coach, Tom, soon after the onset of my six-week heart attack. While he didn't know it at the time (as I was too embarrassed to mention my anxiety), Tom's influence was a major factor in my return to health (in addition to growing my business faster than it had in years).

On our first call, just days after my anxiety had returned, Tom and I started working on a massive 90-day project. Each week we had a phone call check-in on Wednesday afternoon, but little did he know that every time I'd get on the phone with him, I was saying to myself: *Don't freak out. Don't freak out. Don't freak out.* It never happened. There were no full-blown anxiety attacks on any of those calls, but the fear of it ran always through my mind.

In hindsight I now see that talking with Tom was actually a *solution* to my anxiety, not a contributor. Being able to share my problems, even if they were only related to business, allowed me to unclutter the junk in my head. I describe being overwhelmed as having 1000 jigsaw puzzle pieces in your head. If you just leave them there, your mind feels 'scrambled'. The solution is to open up the 'box', spread them out on the table, and then start putting them together so that you have clarity on your thoughts. Getting out of your own head and talking to somebody is one of the best ways to do this, and to reduce your anxiety, and I'll be discussing that (and other solutions) in exact detail later in the book.

Anxiety: The Force Awakens

According to the American Psychological Association anxiety is "an emotion characterized by feelings of tension, worried thoughts and physical changes like increased blood pressure.

People with anxiety disorders usually have recurring intrusive thoughts or concerns. They may avoid certain situations out of worry."[4]

So what causes anxiety? What's the difference between being stressed and having a full-blown attack? How does life go from "overwhelmed" to "sense of impending doom?"

It's impossible to say exactly why one person will experience anxiety attacks while another can be remain calm and carry on under the same circumstances.

Just as some people are more prone to diabetes or cancer, many of us have a greater risk of anxiety. For now, there's nothing you can do about the genetic component. That leaves lifestyle as the battleground for our mental health.

Earlier I mentioned that my anxiety stemmed from being able to do whatever I wanted, whenever I wanted, which became a "Paradox of Freedom." I was in a fortunate position of being successful enough to be my own boss. This meant working as much as I wanted to (which often was 12+ hour days because I was caught up in the rush of making money), or as little as I wanted to (on those hungover mornings after another night out celebrating my success). This paradox of freedom and lack of structure is what led to my downfall.

That might seem strange, to think that more structure is the antidote to anxiety. But make no mistake, this paradox of structure was, and has been, a key to my true and lasting freedom from anxiety. As the author Paulo Coelho puts it, "Discipline and freedom are not mutually exclusive but mutually dependent because otherwise, you'd sink into chaos." That's exactly what happened to me. I sunk into chaos, living through my own special hell, and discovered the hard way – so that you don't have to – that putting more structure into your life will actually help you avoid and overcome anxiety.

When I began living proactively with structure, instead of reactively, I immediately experienced less anxiety and more freedom. In fact, this was such a positive and impactful shift in my life, I wrote a book about how to accomplish the same for you. It's titled *The Perfect Day Formula: How to Own the Day and Control Your Life,* and after you finish this book, I highly recommend getting a copy at FreePerfectDayBook.com

Adrenaline: Nature's Gasoline For Your Anxiety Fire

Remember the scene in Pulp Fiction where John Travolta plunges the needle straight into Uma Thurman's heart, bringing her back to life? That needle was filled with adrenaline—the common name for epinephrine (a hormone and neurotransmitter). Adrenaline is associated with the fight-or-flight response your body experiences when you're scared or surprised, like when you stumble across a black bear in the woods or an intruder in your back yard (which hopefully wasn't where you found the black bear).

When you go to Starbucks for your daily fix, or when you chug a Red Bull (or seven), the caffeine in those drinks stimulates the release of adrenaline, helping to keep you awake.

But too much adrenaline can get you into trouble, and start your mind racing, which is why you might feel overwhelmed when you've had too much coffee or too many Red Bulls. Nicotine, cocaine, and other stimulants also increase the release of adrenaline and can get you into serious trouble.

Too much adrenaline also contributes to anxiety. It stimulates us when we just want to calm down. It keeps us up when we just want to sleep. If you've ever played a sport or done a hard workout too close to bedtime, you're familiar with your body's battle between states of exhaustion and alertness. It's adrenaline that contributes to the latter.

But what most people don't know is that improper breathing also can increase adrenaline, and thus anxiety.

While anxiety is a mental health issue, much of it can be controlled with proper breathing as well as proven and unique strategies for diet and exercise, as we'll discuss later. For now, just realize that your actions, the chemicals you ingest, and how you structure your day are all physical aspects of life that you can control and use to reduce your risk of stress and anxiety.

My Secret Weapon: Introspection

Anxiety attacks will serve as a harsh wake-up call if you've been making some bad decisions. Up until 2006 I had wandered through life relatively unscathed. Sure, I didn't have a perfect childhood (as I'll mention in a moment), but the irony is that I had everything going my way in life when I started suffering from my anxiety attacks.

Perhaps my early business success left me a little too cocky and confident, thinking life was always going to be easy. Money came relatively quickly to me (not that I was Mark Zuckerberg or anything, but only a small number of business owners ever hit seven figures in revenue, let alone at such a young age).

I thought everything was going to go my way forever. But when I was hit with a six-week heart attack, I realized everything had to change. Fortunately, just as in every hero's journey, this inciting incident led me to a life-changing discovery. In my case, the wake-up call led me to the art of introspection, and eventually to my long-term freedom from anxiety and the ability to share this message with millions of people around the world who need a solution to stress and anxiety.

According to Dictionary.com, introspection is defined as "the examination or observation of one's own mental and emotional processes." It's a key to success in many areas of life, from growing your business to creating deep personal relationships. But to be introspective, you must make time for reflection. This might be through meditation, talk therapy, journaling, or writing a book about your experiences. Or it can simply mean sitting and thinking. You might resist this, especially as a hard-charging entrepreneur who might think you don't have time for such "soft" approaches in life. That's why we'll dive deeper in this book to show you how anyone, no matter how busy (or skeptical) they are, can make time for these habits that protect you against anxiety and make you more successful in life.

Introspection works because it helps you connect the dots in life. If you take X action, and then Y happens, you can use that knowledge to change your behavior. If Y is undesirable, and it only occurs when you do X action, then you simply change or eliminate X.

Here's a simple, yet instructive example. Soon after I started being more introspective, it didn't take me long to realize I felt anxiety in the mornings (my undesirable Y) because I was getting up late at 7:30 a.m. (my X action). Because I'm a natural morning person, there were many things I wanted to accomplish before lunch: I wanted to write for an hour, meditate, walk the dog, exercise, eat breakfast while reading interesting books or articles, and yes, at some point, check my email.

Waking up at 7:30 a.m. doesn't allow me to accomplish everything I'd like to do in the morning. This realization alone gave me anxiety. When I recognized this, it became obvious that my actions had to change if I wanted to experience a different outcome (feeling less stressed).

That's when I began getting up five minutes earlier every day, until I eventually settled into my perfect wake-up time thanks to this introspective trial and error.

Over time, and applying introspection to every aspect of my morning, afternoon, and evening activities, I was able to build my perfect day (for productivity, health, wealth, and my social self) and to build a system to overcome my anxiety and prevent it from coming back.

After implementing the strategies in this book and finally returning to an anxiety-free life, I realized I had to share my system with the world. Helping end high-performance anxiety is my new mission in life. I soon began coaching my friends and fellow entrepreneurs on productivity, time management, and reducing stress levels, all while helping them grow their businesses faster than ever.

What I found along the way was that the methods we used to reduce anxiety can be applied to many other aspects of life.

It all comes down to a few critically important, deeply introspective questions. What are you doing right now? What result is that behavior giving you? What is the most impactful thing you can change to reduce your stress and increase your success?

These questions serve as the backbone for the rest of the book, which details the strategies I've uncovered through personal experimentation. This is what has worked for me and my clients, has helped us get through hell, and to become Unstoppable in business and in life.

OK Great, Now What?

There are three vital components in the formula for reducing and preventing anxiety.

The first section, Part One, *Attack Your Anxiety*, provides a platform for taking back control of your mind by aligning your goals and your actions with what really matters to you in life. Then, you can organize your life for more success and less stress. The chapters in Part One are critical to becoming Unstoppable because they provide the focus and foundation you need for the remaining chapters to work.

Next, in Part Two, *Mastering Unstoppable Habits*, you'll discover powerful routines to keep anxiety away, so you can meet the goals you set in Part One. Chapters Four, Five, and Six feature proven approaches to nutrition and exercise, breathing and sleeping, and yoga and meditation. These are the daily building blocks you need to begin eliminating anxiety immediately and setting yourself up for an anxiety-free life.

Part Three, *Being Unstoppable Every Day* is the ultimate blueprint to keeping anxiety away for good. Beating anxiety is a journey, your hero's journey, and something you have to work on every day. You'll learn why surrounding yourself with the right influencers, focusing on others instead of yourself, striving to be more generous, and adopting an attitude of gratitude are needed to become Unstoppable in every area of life.

Finally, I want to talk to you about paying it forward. In the conclusion, *Giving Back*, you'll learn how you can achieve even more when you focus on helping others. Not only does this approach make you more successful in life, it will also be a big breakthrough to escaping anxiety forever.

Your hero's journey to overcoming anxiety starts today. If you follow the simple solutions found in these chapters, you'll learn to control how you feel, and you should never need to worry about having another anxiety attack.

For now, remember these words: *there is nothing wrong with you*. You can and will conquer anxiety with the right tools, a clear path, and an experienced guide to help you on your hero's journey.

This book holds every tool you'll need to lead a happy, successful, anxiety-free life. I will be your guide, and I will show you the path to becoming Unstoppable.

Let's begin.

---

[1] Alex Williams, "Prozac Nation is Now the United States of Xanax," The New York Times, June 10, 2017, accessed September 7, 2018, https://www.nytimes.com/2017/06/10/style/anxiety-is-the-new-depression-xanax.html.

[2] Touré, "Adele Opens Up About Her Inspirations, Looks and Stage Fright," Rolling Stone, April 28, 2011, accessed September 7, 2018, https://www.rollingstone.com/music/music-news/adele-opens-up-about-her-inspirations-looks-and-stage-fright-79626/.

[3] Gene N. Landrum, Paranoia & Power: Fear & Fame of Entertainment Icons (New York: Morgan James, 2007).

[4] "Anxiety," American Psychological Association, accessed May 21, 2018, http://www.apa.org/topics/anxiety.

ATTACK YOUR ANXIETY

Anxiety attacks are called that for a reason: they attack your mind, your body, and your ability to function at 100 percent of your capacity.

You can't put a band-aid on anxiety, ignore it, or run and hide, hoping it will get better. It won't. You have to attack it right back, head on.

How do you attack anxiety? It starts with getting alignment for your mind, structure for your life, and accountability for your actions.

Part One begins with Chapter One, *Unstoppable Alignment*. This chapter reveals the number one factor causing stress in your life: misalignment between your actions and your goals. You'll fix this problem by creating a clear set of values and a North Star vision so that you align your behaviors with your goals.

In Chapter Two, *Unstoppable Structure*, you'll learn how to design your life to protect you from anxiety while supporting your dreams.

In Chapter Three, *Unstoppable Accountability*, I'll share with you a missing link in success, and explain how being accountable to the right people will keep you aligned, support your structure, and reduce your anxiety so you can focus on what's important and achieve greater results in every area of life.

CHAPTER 1

UNSTOPPABLE ALIGNMENT

"You cannot consistently perform in a manner which is inconsistent with the way you see yourself."

— ZIG ZIGLAR

My client, Jack, was very clear about what mattered to him. "Craig," he said, "the most important thing in my life is to raise well-adjusted kids."

It took my brain a second to comprehend what he said. Jack, the guy who worked six days a week, nearly twelve hours a day (not including the commute), was telling me that his family was his number one priority in life? You can probably guess how this was turning out.

Jack was misaligned. His work habits were causing stress at home. His wife felt overwhelmed and unheard. He rarely saw his kids.

Anxiety Starts Here

Jack's not an isolated case. Nearly everyone is misaligned in some area of life. When I was a fitness expert, I saw this nearly every day in the gym. One time I was hired to train the head coach of Toronto's favorite sports team. "Coach" would come in, tell me he wanted to lose twenty pounds, and then proceed to tell me about all the wine he drank and cheese he ate on the post-game plane ride home, and wonder why he wasn't getting anywhere. His actions were not aligned with his goals.

After I wrote my first book, *The Perfect Day Formula*, I began to hear stories from readers who said they wanted to write a book too, but when asked how often they sat down to write, the answer was always, "Oh, I don't have time." Every day I hear from people, many of them high-performers in most areas of life, that want to get up early and attack the day, but who spent hours in bed each night watching television shows, and then the first hour of every morning scrolling through their phone.

This misalignment between actions and goals causes stress, frustration, fear, and failure. Think for a moment where you want to achieve results, whether at work, in the gym, or in your personal life, and then look at your daily actions. Are these actions moving you towards—or away from—your goals? Are you aligned or misaligned?

For years I was as guilty of this as anyone. I wanted to become a world-renowned fitness expert and help millions of people lose weight, get back in shape, and improve their health. But come Friday and Saturday night, I was binge-drinking and acting incongruently with my goals. In fact, I was so mis-aligned and hypocritical that this contributed heavily to my anxiety attacks. It wasn't until I went through my personal hell, restructured my life, and aligned my actions with my goals that I was finally able to have a massive impact on the world, helping millions of people through my books and videos to achieve their goals.

In order to see progress, to reduce stress, and to overcome anxiety, you must align your behaviors and your desires. Bring-ing alignment to your life accelerates your success, focuses your time and resources on what matters most, and helps you achieve your goals. Ultimately, you become an Unstop-pable goal achiever and you overcome your anxiety, fears, and frustrations.

But before you can align attain alignment of your actions and your goals, you first have to identify where your misalignment lies.

What is misalignment, anyway? In the simplest terms, it's what happens when you want one thing but you're chasing something else—like Jack wanting to raise well-adjusted kids, but only making time for work. When misalignment occurs, it creates stress. When realignment occurs, you reduce stress. It's that simple, but you can only accomplish this when you know your values and your vision, when you set your sights on what matters to you (rather than what matters to others, or society's expectations), and when you have accountability to a mentor that keeps you on track.

Don't feel bad if there is misalignment somewhere in your life. This situation is extremely common, and in fact I've never met a person that was 100 percent aligned in every area of life. However, the degree to which each person is misaligned and the stress it causes varies greatly. So what causes people to get so out of line?

First World Problems

This image, the #1 Cause of Friction in Life, depicts how misalignment most commonly shows up in our lives.

Misalignment most often starts with comparison syndrome. This is when you compare yourself to other people and start to believe you need to do what they do, have what they have, and be more like they are – classic first world problems.

We've all heard the saying, "The grass is always greener on the other side." When we think other people's lives are better than ours and we change our actions or our goals to align with someone else's values, we feel stress and anxiety. This can happen in your personal life, such as when you buy a car that's beyond your budget to impress your friends, or in business, like when you see your competitor advertising in a certain place and you think you should be advertising there too.

However, you have limited information about your friends and your competitors. Perhaps your friends went deep in debt to afford their new car, and now they are three months behind on their mortgage because they're spending all their money on car payments.

Your competitor may be advertising at a loss to gain new customers. That may be their current strategy. It may be working but it may not be working, and you have no way of knowing that. The truth is, you have no context for what your friends and your competitors are doing, and it makes no sense for you to blindly follow their lead.

I know, because I learned this lesson the hard way. A few years back, I lost over $250,000 and gained a ton of stress from a bad decision based solely on "what everyone else was doing." At the time, my business was still concentrated in the health and fitness world. Many of my colleagues and competitors began offering cookbooks to their customers using a "free plus shipping" model (where the book was "free", and all the customer had to do was pay a small shipping and handling fee).

I went out and partnered with a chef. I hired five new team members. I invested hundreds of thousands of dollars in the project. And it failed. Why? Well, let me tell you something funny. During the yearlong process of building this new business I was living in a condo in Denver, Colorado. Guess how many times I cooked at home with recipes from the book? Zero. I didn't even turn the stove on once in the time that I lived there. I didn't, and still don't care at all about cooking or cookbooks. The project was completely misaligned with my goals, yet I was chasing this shiny object because "everyone else was doing it." Eventually, I smartened up, cut my (significant) losses, and had to lay off five people in one day. It was the worst day of my career, but this painful situation taught me a valuable lesson: **The grass is greenest when you water it. Live in alignment with *your* values, *your* mission, and *your* goals. Everything else is just noise.**

The bigger lesson is this: your values and your vision are not the same as your friend's or your competitor's. They have different goals and dreams than you, and if you took the time to think about what was truly important in your life (introspection!), you'd realize what matters in your life is not keeping up with your friends or copying your competitors. And since other people's goals do not align with who you are and what you want, you will never be happy chasing them, or even if you obtain them. Instead, you'll simply end up further from your own goals and further misaligned, stressed, and anxious.

How Being Good Makes It Worse

Another cause of misalignment is positive reinforcement. That may seem counterintuitive, because you've probably always equated positive reinforcement with good behavior. However, if you are positively reinforced for behavior that is not in line with your values and vision, and you direct your life toward more of that behavior to obtain more positive reinforcement, you will end up further from your values, vision, and goals, and again, further misaligned, stressed, and anxious.

Positive reinforcement happens in your personal and professional life. For example, perhaps as a teen you started lifting weights to gain muscle mass and dieting to get rid of body fat. You would have received lots of positive reinforcement from your buddies who told you how great you looked. Girls started looking at you differently, too, and that made you feel good. You started spending more time in the gym, restricting your diet further, and loading up on supplements. A fellow bodybuilder pulled you aside in the locker room and told you about some pills he had that could really boost your progress, so you started taking them. At some point, you passed your goal of building mass and lowering your body fat and your lifestyle and diet became obsessive and abnormal. You carry Tupperware food containers with you everywhere you go, and your strict adherence to this regimen prevents you from eating at restaurants or having a social life. The changes seemed so gradual that you didn't even notice them. One day, you look in the mirror, realize this is not who you want to be, and ask yourself (like the old Talking Heads song goes), "How did I get here?"

I felt this way during my anxiety attacks. For years I had received positive reinforcement for binge drinking from my old friends. And although I knew better, this positive reinforcement kept me stuck in a vicious cycle of working hard and living healthy during the week, and then giving in to peer pressure and drinking excessively on the weekend, simply because my buddies rewarded me for doing so. Eventually, this misalignment in my life caused it all to come crashing down in the form of crippling anxiety attacks, something that likely could have been avoided had I stayed true to my values and vision.

Giving in to positive reinforcement without examining the behaviors for which you're receiving it and identifying whether these behaviors are in line with your values, vision, and goals is a slippery slope toward misalignment, that will inevitably lead to stress and anxiety... Likely, you will not even be aware of this because you think you're doing everything right, or at the very least what you are doing is harmless, because hey, nothing bad has happened from it in the past (at least that's how I viewed my drinking problem).

Here's a real-world example that is likely very applicable to your life right now. As an entrepreneur, you probably work a lot of hours and receive praise about your work ethic from your customers, colleagues, and business associates. However, if putting in all those hours at work is moving you away from a higher priority in your life, should you continue that behavior? Think about Jack, my client from the start of this chapter. Sure, his business was more successful than ever (doing over $50 million per year), but he never saw his family, and his number one goal, raising well-adjusted kids, was at risk.

There are plenty of examples from my life where I've made this mistake (which is why I feel so qualified to talk about it). Just after the cookbook fiasco, I found myself wanting to make amends, and to prove my commitment to the business to the rest of my team. I vowed to be the first one in and the last one out of the office every day. The problem was that we allowed our team members to work on a flexible schedule so that they could avoid Denver's growing traffic jams. One of our team members arrived as early as 7 a.m., while another left as late as 6 p.m. That meant me being in the office from

6:30 a.m. to 6:30 p.m., all in the name of "always being there." I was eating every meal in the office, sacrificing sleep (because I had to work out at 5 a.m. so I could be "first in"), and most importantly, surrendering my social life and destroying my dating life (which misaligned me with one of my most important goals, getting married and having a family). My actions did not align with my goals, but I found myself stuck in another vicious cycle of getting positive reinforcement for actions that did not serve me in life.

Misalignment leads to bad decisions and more first-world problems like buying stuff you don't really want or need, behaving in ways that are bad for your health, or working too many hours. Is your vision in life to become a lonely, anxious, stressed out, debt-ridden entrepreneur? Yeah, I didn't think so. Yet, that's exactly where you will end up if you're misaligned and seeking positive reinforcement for actions that do not serve you.

The Paradox of Freedom Putting You in Prison

Misalignment between my actions and my goals created anxiety in my life for years. I knew how hypocritical it was to be preaching personal discipline all week long and engaging in destructive activities every weekend. Getting up at 4:30 in the morning six days a week and then going to bed at 4:30 on a Sunday morning eventually catches up with you. The misalignment in my life and unshakable feeling of being a "two-faced" started to take a physical, mental, and emotional toll that I never expected.

Even though I was writing for *Men's Health* magazine (the biggest fitness publication in the world), selling my workout programs to hundreds of people each day through my website, and training celebrities, doctors, and lawyers, at an exclusive health club in Toronto, I couldn't bring myself to take my own medicine and actually practice what I preached.

Living downtown in Toronto's club district made it all too easy to give into the temptation of going out whenever I wanted (which was pretty much every night of the week) I would regularly go out drinking three nights a week, feebly attempting to hide my hangover during Friday morning sessions with clients, all the while knowing that I would repeat my transgressions later that night. Do you know what the craziest part is? This lifestyle actually worked... For a while.

As my online fitness business grew and I did less and less personal training, this led to a double-edged sword of success gave me even more freedom to do whatever I wanted, whenever I wanted. All structure in my days was thrown out the window because I had fewer people to answer to and nowhere to be at a specific time each day.

It was what I thought I wanted, and what everyone thinks they want—Ultimate Freedom. But this level of autonomy can become a trap. Having complete independence may sound wonderful, but for most people, it leads to bad decisions about how you spend your time, giving in to too much work or too much play. I did both—working all hours of the day and night and partying hard several days a week. My diet suffered, my workouts suffered, my sleep suffered, and I was so out of line that my anxiety, for now, just simmering below the surface, was getting ready to explode.

Misalignment caused by this paradox of freedom isn't reserved for entrepreneurs. It can affect anyone. The boxer Mike Tyson won $300 million in career earnings and he spent it all because he suffered from the paradox of freedom. He was surrounded with "Yes Men", and there was no one around him to say, "No Mike, you can't buy the tiger, Mike." Without boundaries or accountability, he went bankrupt. The actor Johnny Depp put himself in a similar situation, nearly going bankrupt despite earning nearly $20 million per movie. At one point Depp was spending 30 thousand dollars a month on wine. He also reportedly spent $3 million dollars on his friend, Hunter S. Thompson's, funeral. Prince and Michael Jackson had no one enforcing boundaries and guiding them away from the prescription medications that were killing them. With no limits, no boundaries, and no accountability, the paradox of freedom can leave you stressed, broke, or even dead.

You'll also find the paradox of freedom on every college campus, where young people—accustomed to a life of structure imposed on them by their parents—are suddenly given free rein to do whatever they want. Halfway through their freshman year, they realize they're overweight, out of shape, in debt, and failing all their courses. For many, this is their first experience with the paradox of freedom, and one of the many reasons that anxiety is at an all-time high in young people.

But most important, the paradox of freedom has the greatest effect on hard-working entrepreneurs, specifically those that come from modest means (like I did) and think they need to do everything themselves. Your success becomes your curse. As your business grows, more opportunities come your way. You get offers to work on new projects at work, and to take once-in-a-lifetime vacations. You say "YES" to everything, take on far too many new responsibilities, over-promise your time personally and professionally, and slowly but surely the ultimate freedom you once sought becomes a paradoxical prison of misalignment, anxiety, and stress. The good news is that there is a way out, and you hold the key.

Why Do We Get So Much Misery From Being So Misaligned?

Anxiety from misalignment can happen to anyone, but entrepreneurs may be particularly susceptible for a number of reasons. As a business owner, you might believe that no one can do the work as well as you can, so you take on more hustle than you can handle. Rather than make the short-term investment of time to hire and train someone, you continue to do everything yourself, and you suffer the long-term pain of scrambling to run the business alone. You work harder and longer. You eat at your desk, sleep less, and skip date nights, all because you refuse to ask for help or admit that you *can't* do it all.

Does this sound like you? That probably describes every entrepreneur at some time. Even if you do hire people, you're still reluctant to turn over the lion's share of the work, so now you're dealing with all of your original stress, plus you have the added anxiety that comes with managing team members. You absorb your stress, their stress, and the stress of running the business, and you don't share this stress with anyone. Instead, you suffer in silence, thinking you can grind and hustle your way through the worst of it.

Men suffer in silence because that's the manly thing to do. Women suffer in silence because they're supposed to be as strong as their male counterparts and oh, by the way, after they put in a ten-hour day at work, society still expects them to clean the house, cook dinner, do the laundry, and help the kids with their homework, too. But it is simply unsustainable for any entrepreneur, man or woman, to suffer in silence.

The gender issue is worth discussing further. I've worked with female entrepreneurs who run million-dollar businesses while their husbands struggle with this inversion of the gender roles. It's emasculating. Most men were raised to believe it was their job to support the family, yet they're staying home with the kids while their wife is jetting off to business meetings.

This man's old-school dad might point out that his son is not doing his duty of supporting the family—he's washing dishes and changing diapers. Likewise, the old-school mom may be quick to point out that her entrepreneur daughter's housework isn't quite up to par.

Raised to fit one role and trying to fit into this new world is enough to cause anyone tremendous stress. Add to that the responsibility of running your own business, along with the typical go-go personality of an entrepreneur, and it's easy to see where so much of our stress and anxiety comes from.

How to Avoid These Traps

Comparison syndrome, positive reinforcement, and the paradox of freedom all played a part in my misalignment. Thankfully, since becoming aware of these phenomena, I see them for what they are and can avoid the traps.

I won't say that I'm never tempted anymore, though. For example, many of my friends are *really* into cars. They take a lot of pride in owning them, driving them, restoring them, and talking about them. For example, Bedros Keuilian, one of my best friends, business partners, and coaching clients, absolutely loves his Nissan GTR, his restored 1967 Chevelle, and the other goodies he has parked in his private garage. There's nothing wrong with that, because he truly loves those cars and they hold great meaning for him. The problem, though, is when I'm listening to him talk about his cars, I start to feel like I need a really nice car, too. Plus, I've been eyeing a Maserati Granturismo for years. I can afford it, so why not?

Well, I live in a big city, Toronto, and between Uber and walking, I can get to any place I want without driving. I also travel a lot. If I owned a car, I'd end up storing it at the airport for weeks at a time, paying obscene amounts of money in long-term parking fees.

Taking all of that into consideration, why bother with all the hassles of owning a car? Just so I can take some show-off photos for social media? When I think about it that way, the answer is obvious. It's not in line with my values, vision, or my needs, for that matter. Buying a fancy car doesn't make sense for me at all, and if I did give in to comparison syndrome (buying a pricey new car), which in all likelihood would be fortified by positive reinforcement ("Great car, Craig!") I might feel pretty good about it for a minute, but the decision would be out of line from what really matters to me, and the ultimate result would be stress and anxiety.

It's easy to see how quickly comparison syndrome can lead to misalignment in your personal and your professional life. But it's also easy to see how a little introspection and self-reflection on your values and vision can keep you off this slippery slope of bad decisions and anxiety-inducing mistakes. When you can stick to the right path for your right life, you become Unstoppable and achieve success faster than ever.

The Phrase That Pays

Alignment begins with getting crystal clear about what matters to you most in life, personally and professionally. As I like to say, "Your values and vision drive every decision." This is the phrase that pays off when you live it in the long run. When you know where you want to go in life you can design a simple straight line to success that gets you there fast while preventing you from going on dangerous detours.

Your values are the cornerstone of your alignment and are best described as the things that matter the most to you in terms of your health, wealth, relationships, and experiences. Your vision is how you picture yourself living life in accordance with those values.

When you have your values and your vision, it becomes easy for you to make the right decisions because the path to success is so clearly laid out.

In the following exercises, you'll define your own values and envision a life that supports those values. When you put these thoughts down into words on paper you can finally begin to create the kind of structure in your life that leads to alignment. This framework, built on what matters to you most, will make it easier for you to make the right decisions to live your right life.

Exercise: Build Your Values Pyramid

Please answer the following questions.

What are the greatest accomplishments you want to achieve in the next ten years for your top values in life:

- Your Family?

- Your Health?

- Your Wealth?

- Your Experiences?

For example, here are my answers:

- Family: Have a wife and two (or more) amazing children

- Health: Feel like I'm 17 forever

- Wealth: $5 million income and an annual donation of $1,000,000 to Toys for Tots, Shriners Hospital, and Medical Missions

- Experiences: Write 3 more books that have as big of an impact as The Perfect Day Formula

These values, clearly and concisely defined, guide every decision I'll make in my life. If I want to feel like I'm 17 forever, that means exercising regularly (and doing my "old-man warm-up" every time so I remain injury-free). It also means putting my dating life ahead of my desire to take on new work projects (something I often found difficult to do in the past prior to completing this exercise). Doing this exercise is the first step in becoming more aligned in your daily actions and what really matters to you in life.

Build Your Vision on Your Values

Once you've completed the values pyramid exercise, you can create a vision for your life based on your values. I want you to create this vision writing from a date three years in the future and describing exactly what you have accomplished.

I refer to creating your vision as writing the "movie script" of your life. Your vision should be so clear and so specific that when you read it to me, I can picture your future in my mind just as easily as I can watch a movie on a screen.

For example, say your highest value is your family life. Your vision for this value might be "being a strong father or mother who spends two hours every evening with my children, every Sunday with my family, and taking my spouse on a date once night a week." Your vision provides clarity on what matters, provides boundaries for your behaviors, and prevents you from doing things that do not serve you.

Here's the vision I've created for my future life:

"It's June 20th, 2021. Father's Day. I'm in the backyard at 35 Sir Adam Beck Drive in Stratford, Ontario, Canada, with my family, my friends, and my business partners and their families. It's a beautiful sunny day and you can feel the warm breeze and smell hamburgers cooking as we gather around the pool. Bedros Keuilian, one of my best friends, is working the grill. The kids are running around the pool, and of course, one of the parents is yelling, 'Stop running around the pool.' We're celebrating Father's Day, and the phenomenal growth in my coaching business. We're celebrating our clients, too, and all the success we've helped them achieve. Life has been good for me, my family, friends, and my clients, and am so thankful for all of it.

In the last three years, I've achieved some major goals. I've moved our family to our forever home. I have sold 250,000 copies of my books. My $10 million business now has 3,000 students enrolled in our coaching programs each year.

My family travels on vacation three times per year, to Florida in the winter and to Denver in December, where we host our annual 'Toys for Tots' charity drive. My wife and I have a date night every week, we volunteer one weekend a month at our favorite charity, and we're very involved with our children's activities. And every Sunday, we commit to a Device-Free Family day, putting away our electronics so we can focus on being present with each other."

Can you picture the movie of my life with that description? Can you see it, feel it, hear it, and even smell it? The clarity in my vision is the secret ingredient to making my dream life come true. Perhaps there are some similarities between it and the life you envision for yourself? Of course, everyone's vision is different, because your values, goals, and dreams are different from mine. This is why you have to define your own as clearly as possible.

When you create your vision with as much specificity as I have above, you'll have what I call the dream destination for your life. It outlines the life you want to lead and describes the person you wish to become, and with this North Star guiding you, you'll make the right decisions every day so that you can achieve exactly what you want in life. That path allows you to say no to detours and distractions that bring misalignment, stress, and anxiety. When you have strong values and a clear and concise vision for your life, you can focus on what matters and say no to what does not, and you become so aligned with your actions and your goals that you become Unstoppable.

Exercise: Create Your Perfect Life Vision

Writing out the vision for your life is one of the most important things you can do to eliminate the clutter in your head and put you on a clear path to success.

If you need more space, write in a notebook or type up your perfect life vision on your computer. Get it in writing so you can see what it looks like. Sleep on it and then make changes to it tomorrow. As you gain clarity around your values, update your life's vision on an annual basis.

1. The date is:

2. The location is:

3. I am with:

4. We are celebrating:

5. In the past three years we have:

6. Big Accomplishment #1:

7. Big Accomplishment #2:

8. Big Accomplishment #3:

9. Our family does this:

10. My partner and I do this:

11. Each year we:

12. We participate in:

Action Beats Anxiety

There's a reason why top entrepreneurs and executives hire me for a full day to work on their values and vision. It takes time, focus, and big thinking. Although it sounds simple, it's not easy. Here's how to start. Set aside thirty minutes on a Saturday morning to list your values and write your vision, and keep refining both to give you clarity, and help you overcome your feelings of being overwhelmed. This will give you momentum to live on your own terms, suffering from less comparison syndrome and anxiety, and getting closer to your big goals and dreams every day. (If you struggle with this and need my help, send me an email at Craig@Godfather.com.)

If you're sitting on the couch reading this book and worrying, spinning the wheels in your mind about how you're going to get aligned, you need to do something about it now.

Here's an analogy I often use at my workshops. Picture yourself as a Formula One Race Car, an amazing machine with a high-powered engine, yet you are stuck in mud spinning your wheels. You can step on the gas all you want, but without, you go nowhere. The job of the values and vision exercise is to give you clarity, essentially lifting you up, and placing your wheels back on the road, where you can drive off at 200 mph in the right direction on the fast track to success.

But if you don't take time to step back and align your actions with your values and your vision, you'll remain stuck, stressed and anxious.

Put this book down for a moment of introspection. Imagine yourself 30,000 feet up in the air looking down on your life, and at your behaviors contributing to your overwhelming feelings of confusion and misalignment.

What do you see here in the big picture? Is there one major factor that needs to change for you to be in alignment? Perhaps you're living in the wrong town or hanging out with the wrong people. You might be living hypocritically, as I once did. You may even be chasing the wrong goals in life, going after money or "stuff" or certain relationships because of society's pressure when in fact these so-called goals don't matter to you at all. These are potentially big issues, granted, but it is within your power to change them. Think about these things, the stress that they cause, and make a conscious commitment to changing your ways and your situation in life to reduce your stress so you can have more success. With this knowledge, we can put in place a plan for creating harmony between your actions and your life's vision, a vision built on clarity, so that you can become aligned and leave anxiety behind.

Next, close your eyes and choose one small item or action in your life—just one—that's out of line and causing you anxiety. Identify one small step toward eliminating that misalignment and alleviating some of that stress right now.

Taking one small step in the right direction is much more effective than sitting around worrying about it. Ask yourself, "What can I do in the next twenty-four hours—or even right now—to overcome my feelings of being overwhelmed in life?" Choose that path and take action.

For example, you could alleviate some stress at work by finding ways to delegate tasks on your enormous—and overwhelming—to-do list. Is there something you do within your business that you could hire someone else to do? Identify one or several jobs, then go online and see how much it would cost for a virtual assistant, copywriter, video editor, bookkeeper, or some other professional to help you out. Then do the same for the stressful items in your personal life. How much would it cost to delegate your dry cleaning, your meal prep, your lawn care, etc. so that you don't have to worry about the little things every day. Listen, you can't get rich and you can't be successful if you are stressed out and spending your time doing $10-an-hour tasks most of the day. I see this mistake being made all the time in my clients, but making these changes is one of the fastest ways to alleviate day-to-day anxiety and get back on the road to recovery.

The path to becoming Unstoppable starts with taking one small step in the right direction right now so that you become more aligned in life, more successful in business, and less stressed out at home.

Remember the Unstoppable mantra:

Action Beats Anxiety. Motion beats Meditation. Work Beats Worry.

You won't make progress sitting and stewing or waiting and worrying. You'll only make progress when you start doing.

Summary

- Misalignment between you values and vision, and your actions and behavior, causes stress and anxiety. This misalignment may be caused by comparison syndrome, misguided positive reinforcement, and the paradox of freedom. The stress it creates can be felt internally, in overwhelming demands on your time, in strained relationships with your family, financially, and in many other versions of stress that all add up to high anxiety.

- By identifying your values, becoming aware of the activities and habits that are not in line with your values, and replacing them with actions and behaviors that are aligned, you can begin to reduce your anxiety.

- Creating a clear and concise vision for your life is a terrific way to see where you want to go. Envision that life, then close your eyes and recall the day you had today. How do the two versions of your day compare?

- Comparing a day in the life of your perfect vision to the life you have right now will show you the differences, and then you can identify the current behaviors that are preventing you from achieving your vision.

- Alignment may require big-picture changes, but you can start small, and you should start immediately. Remember, my friend: Action beats Anxiety. Motion beats Meditation. Work beats Worry. One step at a time, you become Unstoppable.

CHAPTER 2

UNSTOPPABLE STRUCTURE

"Adhering to a daily schedule that is led by your vision and run by your priorities is the surest path to personal freedom."

– MARK FORD, FOUNDER, EARLY TO RISE

Think back to a day when you were running around like a proverbial chicken with its head cut off. You started late and only got more behind schedule as the day went on, working in reactive mode, putting out fires, responding to email, and getting sucked into social media. You were overwhelmed from minute one and ended the day on the verge of a full-blown anxiety attack. You were active without accomplishment, making no time for priority projects like writing your book, executing on an important marketing plan for your business, or preparing for that big presentation. At six o'clock you sat back and thought, "Where did the day go?"

That night, the worrisome "anxiety earworms" started burrowing deeper into your head. Your mental wheels were turning and turning, revving your anxiety engine faster and faster, thinking of all the work that piled up and got added to tomorrow's to-do list. You toss and turn, unable to slip off to sleep as your mind races with the ever-growing responsibilities and the knowledge that you're making no progress on your big goals and dreams (and probably won't tomorrow, or the next day, or the next day).

After a restless night, you oversleep and so you skip breakfast just to get to work on time, and it's all downhill from there. You struggle to make it through the day, scrolling through emails and jumping from one emergency to the next. Tired and hungry, you finish your work an hour later than usual and you finally make it home—just as your family is finishing dinner.If you remain stuck in this cycle, how long do you think it will be before the   anxiety attacks begin? This is the inevitable penalty when there is no structure in your day, and you don't make time to make progress on the things that matter. If you are always spending time in activity, you'll never make time for accomplishment.

When you end every day without progress on your big goals, you begin to lose momentum. Without momentum, you lack motivation. No motivation, no action. No action, no progress. And the vicious cycle continues.

The antidote to a reactive, anxiety-ridden life is structure. When you have more structure in your life, quite counterintuitively, you actually end up with more freedom through the virtuous cycle of focus, action, results, momentum, and more focus.

Here's how the earlier example would be different, when taking a proactive approach. To begin the day, you wake up earlier than everybody else, and you make time for introspection and to work on what matters. You've planned your day the night before, so that you know exactly what to do in these magic morning minutes and so that you don't waste any precious time in the morning trying to put in place a plan for your day.

You get your highest priority task done before anyone else in the house wakes up. It might be fifteen minutes of preparing for meetings, writing your next book, reading the Bible, or exercising, or even doing meditation or gratitude journaling to set your mind right for the day. (A quick note: I know what you're thinking. *What can I do in fifteen minutes?* Well, as a person who has written three books and built a seven-figure business in short daily increments at 4:30 in the morning, trust me, fifteen minutes of focus on your most important tasks can move you ahead big time in every area of your life. If you can commit to that, you will see progress, gain momentum, and build motivation to keep you moving ahead every morning.)

After getting stuff done on your most important task (*GSD* on your *MIT*), the rest of the house is getting up. Everyone has breakfast, and leaves on time, before traffic gets crazy. You get to work a few minutes early, not feeling rushed or anxious, prepared for a day of accomplishment and progress.

You begin working on your most important task and make massive progress—perhaps even completing it—before you open your email or sneak a peek at social media. You work with focus, taking a few scheduled rest breaks, and at lunch, you make time for a nice walk outside. After a productive afternoon, you plan out the next day, leave work on time, and also leave thoughts of work behind so you can be present with your family and friends at night. You put your phone in another room, so you won't be glued to it all evening. You've won the day and can enjoy your evening.

Your life is productive, balanced, and free of anxiety. Why? Because you have *structure*.

You might roll your eyes at the description and say it's impossible, but it's not. My client Bedros Keuilian, CEO of Fit Body Boot Camp, runs one of the fastest growing franchises in America with nearly 1000 locations. He's up at 5:30 a.m for his morning ritual (including playing fetch with his dog, Cookie), does a block of deep work from 6 a.m. to 9 a.m., then goes to the gym, and is at his office before 11 a.m. for meetings with his team. He leaves no later than 5 p.m. and gets home early to spend time with his kids. After family dinner, he has more time with the kids, an hour to watch a show with his wife, jump in the hot tub, and get to bed before 10:30 p.m. I know because I watch this happen. Bedros and I have been friends for nearly a decade and I've watched him overcome his own anxiety (that also left him thinking he was having a heart attack) and put more structure in his life so he could have more freedom. He did this through what he calls "environmental exposure" to me and by adopting the same unstoppable habits and routines he would see me do each day.

The program also works for busy female entrepreneurs with children. Two of my most successful clients, Shanda Sumpter and Isabel De Los Rios, are up early, they GSD on their MIT, and then have family breakfast time. Both finish their workday before 3 p.m. to make time for their children. Isabel participates in homeschooling her children, all while running an eight-figure health and wellness company, while Shanda has a daily ritual of picking her son up at school at 2:45 p.m. and then taking him for a walk on the beach. They have overcome feelings of anxiety and being overwhelmed because they have more structure in their days.

Building Unstoppable Structure means planning ahead and identifying and eliminating obstacles and temptations that can get in your way, so that you can align your actions with your goals. Once you have that foundation in place, you can create the right environment for getting stuff done on your most important tasks while avoiding time wasters that get you off track—and lead to stress and anxiety.

First World Problem: You Are Overwhelmed With Opportunity

When I talk to entrepreneurs, the word "overwhelmed" comes up often. For the entrepreneur, there is always more to be done.

Your never-ending to-do list, meeting schedule, and desire to balance work and home life can feel chaotic and give you feelings of anxiety. You're responsible for your customer's satisfaction, your employee's income, and your success. And let's face it, your ego, your reputation, and your legacy all weigh heavily on you as well. If you lose a customer or a deal, there are real consequences, and you are directly, sometimes devastatingly, impacted. There is always another email to answer, a contact to make, a social media page to update, a meeting to have, or a contract to review. It's easy to let work bleed into all the other areas of your life. The pressure can feel relentless.

Your busy schedule can quickly become overwhelming, especially if you try to take on every new opportunity. My client, Joe Polish, says, "Entrepreneurs are intoxicated with opportunity." He's right. We're drowning in ideas, potential deals, and new opportunities.

You're like the child at the ice cream store that wants to try every flavor. The more successful you become, the more you attract new opportunities. People want your time, they want to partner with you, and they'll want you to speak at their events. You then have so many directions to go to grow your business, and the fear of missing out drives you to try them all.

I know what it's like, and more importantly, I know the trouble this can bring—especially if other businesses like yours are doing them (there's that comparison syndrome again). But more opportunities simply bring more distractions from what you really should be doing with your time.

We can't do everything. Elon Musk is a living example of the breakdown that is bound to happen when you spread yourself too thin. It's admirable what he's trying to accomplish, but he's human too, and finding out his limits the hard way. Yes, we all must make sacrifices in life. Just make sure you aren't sacrificing the things that are highest on your priority list or taking your energy away from your values and vision.

Time to Look in the Misalignment Mirror

When high performers come to me, one of my biggest jobs is to align their actions with their goals and values. Sometimes this means putting their ambitions in check, and sometimes it mean expanding their minds.

For example, one of my clients, Brian Kalakay, is the owner of two very successful Fit Body Boot Camp locations in Michigan. Like many of us, Brian is influenced by the success stories he sees online, and sometimes his dreams get detoured from what really matters in life. You see, Brian has a young family, and his wife and daughter are his most important value. Sometimes, during his weekly accountability emails to me, I have to correct his direction in life when I notice him working too much or taking on too many new projects.

This serves two purposes: First, it gets his actions aligned with what really matters in his life – family. Second, it actually makes him more successful in business too, because he focuses on what matters rather than chasing shiny objects. Focus, as both Bill Gates and Warren Buffett will tell you, is the key to success – and also to less stress and anxiety.

I learned that the hard way, having lost a lot of money, sleep, and time opening new businesses too fast, or doing something for money instead of for meaning.

Brian and I don't want you to make the same mistake.

The paradox of freedom—being able to do whatever you want, whenever you want—leads to a shotgun-scattered approach to your days and exacerbates your stress and anxiety. It puts you in a prison, and the only way out is to adopt the paradox of structure so that you can finally focus on what matters.

If you're a parent, then you'll likely agree that spending quality time with your kids is one of the most important things in your life.

If you don't have kids, the same desire is often expressed around relationships with a spouse, partner, boyfriend, or girlfriend. You want more meaningful time with them to enjoy life and do the things you love to do. That's the goal. But let's look at your actions. Are you making time for your loved ones in life? And if you're single and want that to change, are you making any time at all for this goal?

For most executives or entrepreneurs, the answer is no. It's not uncommon for high performers to have a problem drawing the line between work and family life. With no boundaries, you inevitably end up spending "YES" to too many shiny objects and new projects, and spending too much time working and too little time on your highest priorities in life. Whether or not you're consciously aware of it, that dichotomy—telling yourself you're a good parent or partner, yet prioritizing work over family—can wreak havoc in your head. You may be ignoring the truth or blind to it, but when your actions are out of line with your values, anxiety builds. Your mind is racing, your head is cluttered, your body is tense, and you may not even know why you're so stressed. The solution, the same one that helped Brian, Bedros, Shanda, and Isabel, is to put more boundaries into your life.

Believe Me, Boundaries Set You Free

Bedros has 97 numbers blocked on his phone. These are the numbers of energy vampires, negative people, gossips, and others whose messages don't serve his purpose. Sounds harsh to some, but it's liberating for him. He no longer loses precious minutes dealing with people who waste his time.

Most people want to resist this idea of hard boundaries, perhaps because you fear other people's judgment, or you mistakenly believe your creativity will suffer under structure. But believe me, boundaries are essential if you want to be free. They allow you to separate work and home life, to get to bed on time, and to avoid bad habits that bring you down.

Daniel Elk, CEO of Spotify, agrees. *"I write out what my daily, weekly, monthly goals are, and every evening I check how I'm doing. And then I allocate my time to match the goals. People think that creativity is this free spirit that has no boundaries. No, actually the most creative people in the world schedule their creativity. That's the irony."*

We all, myself included, spend time on things that are *not* in alignment with the person we want to be, and those activities should be the first to be removed from our daily schedule. Boundaries need to be applied to the amount of time you spend on social media, about how you use your phone when you are at home with your family, about how many Netflix shows you can watch in an evening before bed, and about how many drinks you'll have at dinner.

This is the structure you must apply to your life. It's tempting to resist it, but listen, what you're doing is not working now, you wouldn't be reading this book if it was. When I made the decision to add more structure into my life, to put boundaries around work and play, my stress and anxiety plummeted, as it does for all of my clients that follow this advice.

Setting boundaries includes giving you permission to say "NO" to things that don't matter at work and at home. If you're an entrepreneur, ask yourself if it makes sense to prepare every meal, to run every errand, to do all the household chores, or even to drive yourself to the airport rather than taking a car service. Each of these activities comes with a cost of time, money, and energy, and often trading your money for more time, energy, and freedom is the right decision to make.

Making every meal comes with sacrifices that may be higher priorities for you, like time for exercising, having a meaningful conversation with your spouse, reading to your kids before bedtime, or indulging in a relaxing massage. You might have been raised to think that you don't have to do everything; you can set boundaries around these activities and you can make more time for what matters. We are not living in the same era as when our parents did, when they had to do everything themselves. I give you permission to let go of the guilt and subscribe to a meal plan delivery service or order to-go meals online from your favorite restaurant and have them delivered to your door so that you can focus on what matters—being present—rather than adding another distraction to your day.

When I was battling my anxiety and aligning my life, I had to set boundaries for work and play. It wasn't easy to stick to them at first. I was tempted to work through dinner, to check email "just one more time before bed," or to have a couple of drinks each night at a three-day seminar. But each of these wrong decisions would have led me down a slippery slope of more bad decisions that eventually led to anxiety.

If you don't stick to your rules and boundaries, you'll soon be letting old bad habits creep back into your life and drag you down. If you've made a promise to be present with others and you're sneaking glances at your phone, the people around you will notice. They will become resentful, too, even if they don't say anything about it at first, and simply because *you* know you're doing it, it will start adding to your internal misalignment.

Boundaries can be built. There are no excuses. One of my clients has a rule that all devices must be turned off by eight p.m. Some of my other clients do their best to enjoy screen-free Sundays: no laptop, TV, television, or smartphones. That may be a hard adjustment, but once you've made it a habit, you'll feel unbelievably liberated. You'll look forward to those evenings or days of being totally present with your friends, family, and how you're going to spend your time with them.

In my first book, *The Perfect Day Formula*, I lay out the exact step-by-step process for getting your life in order by controlling your morning, conquering your afternoon, and concentrating on what counts. I recommend you pick up a copy of that book at FreePerfectDayBook.com.

In the meantime, you can kickstart your new, unstoppably structured life with some simple changes to your schedule.

Are You Making This Classic Mistake In The Morning?

As a high-performing person, it's especially important to plan your day the night before. Having a detailed plan of action waiting for you in the morning allows you to get stuff done on your most important tasks immediately. That then allows you to stick to your values and vision and empowers you to say no to anything that's not in alignment with you. It's like setting off a series of dominoes in a positive direction in your life, but that first domino is critical, and it always starts the night before your next perfect day. Remember this saying:

"If you are making your to-do list in the morning, you're already too late!" Effective planning must be done the night before so that you don't waste the most productive time of your day the next morning.

The Little Known Secret to Having a Perfect Day

A daily plan makes it much easier to stick to your boundaries. If one of your rules is to be home by 5:30 to help make dinner for the family, then you know you have to leave work at a certain time in order to keep your promise. Knowing that, you'll have boundaries on the last meeting of your day, when you need to wrap up all of your calls, and when you need to shut down your phone. If you don't have this daily plan and subsequent boundaries, you won't be out of the office by 5 and you won't be home in time for dinner, and that means you'll be stressed and out of alignment with what really matters in your life. A daily plan is a necessity to accomplish anything and everything, from being successful at work to reaching your big goals and dreams.

Erik and Amy, two of my clients, have five kids, a busy coaching business, a love for travel, and a commitment to staying healthy and fit. If the average person looked at their life, they'd be shocked at how Erik and Amy got everything done and lived the Perfect Life. One of the major keys in their success has been the institution of more daily boundaries (around work projects, priorities, and cut-off times) and the use of detailed planning the night before for the day ahead.

When you're creating your workday plan like Erik and Amy do, you need to harness the power of introspection. Sit for a moment and mentally walk through your day and try to account for everything in your plan. This includes commute time, time for making calls, meetings, and everything else that makes up your typical workday. I have a process for this evening planning outlined in a helpful format called the Perfect Day Script, which follows these three steps:

1. Brain Dump: This is where you get everything out of your head (i.e. all those jigsaw puzzle pieces cluttering up your mind). About ten minutes before you leave work each day, jot down a list of all the activities you need to do the following day. Include tasks like responding to emails, working on a presentation, running personal errands, client calls, meetings, and going to the gym. Getting everything out of your head and "on paper" will relieve some stress immediately because it reduces the clutter in your head.

2. Prioritize: Number everything from your brain dump from most to least important. In other words, identify the most critical item on your list and put a #1 next to it, then continue numbering in order of importance. This is your prioritized to-do list (and it's like putting all of the jigsaw pieces together in order). Don't wait until the next day to make this list—do it at the end of your workday, while those tasks are fresh in your mind. That's when

you should be getting stuff done on your most important tasks. As Erik and Amy found out with practice, the more detailed you are in setting your daily plan, the more successful you will be the following day because you won't be wasting time on tasks that aren't aligned with your personal and professional goals.

3. Process Planning: You're probably already doing some form of daily planning, so doing a brain dump and creating a prioritized to-do list should be a fairly easy adjustment. You just need to make sure you do it and do it every day. Set an alarm and get accountability from a friend or mentor if you need it to help stay on track with these powerful new habits. But there's a third step you're probably not doing that will set you up for even greater success, which I call process planning. Process planning is doing something to make the following day's tasks easier. It's like giving yourself a jumpstart on each item. For instance, if you have to create a PowerPoint the next morning, open a template and put a list of bullet points in it of things you want to cover. This will make the assignment less daunting the next day, because you've already got a head start. If you're going to run three miles before breakfast, lay out your clothes beside your bed the night before so you can slip into them quickly and hit the road or trail. As a writer, process planning is the secret ingredient to my success. I can have "write Chapter Three of my book" listed as my most important task for the morning, but if I wake up without having done my process planning and go straight to a blank screen, chances are that I'll have writer's block and start procrastinating.

But if I do just a few minutes of outlining my writing the night before, it sets up my subconscious mind to do the work overnight, and the words just flow out of me the next morning under the influence of my outline. Process planning is the game changer you've been looking for in order to get more done each day.

Using the Perfect Day Script approach puts you in the driver's seat in life, helping you become more proactive and avoiding wasted days where you find yourself in reactive mode. This little known, but simple 3-step system will help you dominate your days and become Unstoppable at work.

NO is Not a Four-Letter Word: Make It Your Mantra

"The difference between successful people and very successful people," Warren Buffett said, "Is that very successful people say 'NO' to almost everything."

Developing the ability to say "no" more often is a superpower that will serve you well and having clear boundaries allows you to turn down requests to do things that may seem like a good idea on the surface but that aren't in alignment with your goals and ultimately do not serve you. Your values, vision, and goals must act as filters for opportunities that come your way. When you're able to say no more often, your stress and anxiety will plummet.

For example, say your top value in life is to spend more time with your family, and so you set a boundary that you don't work on Sundays. Now imagine that you've been asked to speak at an out-of-town convention on Saturday afternoon, which would require you to fly home Sunday morning, missing the first half of the day you've devoted to family. When you run that through a filter of your values and vision, it becomes easy for you to say no. Unless you learn to view opportunities through filters, you'll have a difficult time knowing what to do and what to turn down, and you'll soon be stressed. Having that go-to solution in place for making decisions will reduce your anxiety immensely.

Be the Oprah of Your Business

When I first met Shanda, she was a successful entrepreneur who appeared to be doing everything right. In reality, Shanda was overwhelmed. Stuck in the crossover generation between baby boomer and millennial, she was doing everything society expected of her as a wife and mother, and everything she thought she was supposed to be doing as an entrepreneur.

Shanda wanted to keep being successful in business, but she wanted to be more present for her family, too. When I began working with her, and as we talked about her day-to-day activities and broke down where she was spending her time, we discovered she was chasing many opportunities that weren't in line with her values. For example, Shanda had set up many social media groups, where she answered questions for people who needed the kind of guidance she offered. The problem was, answering all those questions wasn't helping Shanda's family relationships and it wasn't doing much for her business either. Shanda had to learn to give herself permission to not take personal responsibility for every individual's issues, and to step away from those groups.

Consider Oprah, and the demands on her time. If she answered every question from every individual who needed her help, she'd have time for nothing else. Instead, she packed her best advice into a daily one-hour show that reached millions. Sometimes, you think you're doing the right things, but you have to take a step back and look at the big picture. How do your actions impact your goals, and is there a better way?

Shanda brought in other coaches to help her, and instead of answering every individual's questions, she scheduled group calls where people could still have access to her. Instead of running herself ragged at the tactical level of the business, she took on a strategic role, becoming, in effect, the chess master rather than the pawn. This freed her time for other activities, like strategic thinking to grow her business (and help more people), and spending more time with her family.

She stopped playing by other people's rules and put in place her own boundaries that helped put her life back together, properly aligned so that her life was less stressful and more successful. Shanda became unstoppably structured, and reaped the benefits with more time for play, a happier home life, and a bigger and better business. Shanda became the "Oprah" of her business, and you must too.

Exercise: Create Your Perfect Day Script

Think about what you should be doing with your time tomorrow. Imagine your perfect day and script it out.

1. Brain Dump:

2. Prioritize Your List:

    a. What are the most important tasks, activities, or events?

    b. What activities are least important?

3. Process planning: What can you do right now to give yourself a jumpstart on tomorrow?

Summary

- Being overwhelmed is caused by having no boundaries, or boundaries that aren't tight enough, around your values- and vision-aligned goals.

- Setting boundaries and instituting a filtering system empowers you to say no to activities that hinder your progress toward achieving those goals.

- A daily plan facilitates your alignment and structure and provides you with a straight line to success.

CHAPTER 3

UNSTOPPABLE ACCOUNTABILITY

*"If more information were the answer, we'd all be
billionaires with six pack abs"*

— DEREK SIVERS, SERIAL ENTREPRENEUR, FOUNDER CD BABY

Everything you want to know is available for free on YouTube.
No matter what you want to accomplish, there are how-to
videos about making money, losing weight, fixing the toilet,
playing Fortnite or Madden, and even about writing a book.
But if all this information is out there and free to access, why
isn't everyone experiencing fabulous success? For example,
one of my exercise videos from my previous fitness business
has been watched over 3 million times on YouTube. So why
aren't more Americans fit and in shape? Well, it's because
free advice (including mine) has always been missing a secret
ingredient: accountability.

Without accountability, there is no one holding you to your promises, and as such, there are no consequences to you not doing the work. If you wake up with a plan to write a book chapter before noon, you may have every intention of writing that chapter, but chances are you will get distracted. It might even be the highest priority for your day but for some reason you just can't find the motivation to get started. You push it off until after lunch, and after lunch, after even more procrastination and rationalization, you push it off to the next day. And if you have no accountability to anyone about getting it done, then no one knows you failed, there are no consequences, and there's no pain.

That's why public accountability is an incredible motivator. If you declare to the world that you're going to do something, and then you fail to follow through, you're going to look like a hypocrite—and the world hates a hypocrite. But with the secret ingredient of accountability on your side, you can make dramatic changes in your life, become incredibly productive, and achieve enormous success, almost automatically. And even though it seems scary and stressful, public accountability will actually reduce your anxiety.

You can even use accountability to make small, but profound changes in your life. In 2011, I used accountability to quit swearing: I shared my plan with my 150,000 newsletter subscribers for accountability, and decided then and there that I would not let them down. Within five days, I had "cured" myself of cursing. It was that simple, knowing that I had to stick to my word or look like a hypocrite. That's the power of putting accountability to work for you.

Instead of thinking of accountability as a potential threat, see it as an enabler that drives you toward your values, vision, and goals, and moves you away from stress and anxiety

How to Change Your Limiting Self-Beliefs

Limiting self-beliefs, where you mistakenly believe that you're not good enough, smart enough, or worthy enough of success, can stop you from making the necessary changes you need to become Unstoppable. My clients and I often have to spend a day together to make these massive mental shifts, but you can't wait that long. We need to give you fast progress so you can build momentum and motivation right now. One way to change your behaviors fast is to plug into a powerful source of support called accountability. Accountability will motivate you to make changes right away, while you're in the process of changing what you believe about yourself.

Accountability gets you to do those things you think you can't do, or don't have the motivation to do. It will get you to eat an apple instead of Oreos, to get out of bed instead of hitting the snooze button, and to write that speech – or finish that book – instead of cleaning out your inbox. Accountability is a way of having someone else hold you to a higher standard than you hold yourself, so you can break away from those limiting beliefs and labels and do what needs to be done.

For example, even though I'm well known for my habit of getting out of bed at precisely 3:57 a.m. every morning, seven days a week, there are many days when I wake up and am tempted to hit the snooze button. However, first of all, I am accountable to you and to everyone that has ever read my advice to "never hit the snooze button." For that reason alone, I always get out of bed on time. But there's a second source of accountability that moves me to action. It comes from my friend, Bedros, who says, "When you hit the snooze button, you're telling your hopes and dreams that they can wait." After I first heard him phrase it like that in one of his speeches, I resolved immediately to double down on my habit of getting out of bed on time.

Are you surprised to hear that I wanted to hit snooze? Why, because I seem so disciplined? I am disciplined—very disciplined. My clients call me the most disciplined man in the world. But even I need accountability to stay on track – and that's why it's one of the secrets to your success. Accountability makes the difference between wishing and succeeding.

The *Secret*, Secret Ingredient

But wait, there's more! While accountability *is* the secret ingredient to finally following through on what you need to do to reach your goals, there's actually a secret ingredient to this secret ingredient. It goes like this.

You must be accountable to someone that you deeply do not want to disappoint.

Read that again. Write it down. Post it on a sticky note on your computer. Make it the wallpaper image on your iPhone. The person you hold yourself accountable to can't be just anyone— it must be someone you deeply do not want to disappoint. I figured this out early in my own quest for becoming more accountable. I had coaches who urged me to do this or that, and I promised them I would. I understood the benefits to changing my behavior, and I wanted to change, but it was just as easy to not change, or not do what needed to be done. More importantly, I did not care if I let these people down. To become truly accountable, I had to seek out people who I truly did not want to disappoint and make myself accountable to them.

Think about the people you've known throughout your life that you didn't want to disappoint, and the lengths to which you might have gone to satisfy their expectations. Was there a teacher, a pastor, a grandparent, or a coach you respected— someone who believed in you so much, that they helped you believe in yourself, and you never wanted to let them down? This person doesn't have to be someone you pay, like a professional coach, and in fact, it often is not. They simply believe in you and have high expectations of you—probably higher than you have of yourself – and that is what drives you to not disappoint them. It's almost irrational, but when you have this in place you can move mountains in your life.

It may seem counterintuitive that being accountable to someone could reduce your anxiety. However, having people in your life to whom you're accountable will encourage you to stay on track with your values- and vision aligned plan. You'll begin to change what you believe about yourself, make real progress toward your goals, and ultimately, truly align yourself with what you want to do, and who you want to become.

Compare that situation with living a life out of alignment, with no plan and no accountability – or worse, accountability to the wrong people that don't believe in you. Which do you think would be more stressful, and which would be more likely to be anxiety-free?

Like the paradox of freedom that binds you and the paradox of structure that sets you free, the paradox of accountability serves not to create more stress in your life, but to enable you to follow an anxiety-free path toward your goal.

Fail to Plan, Plan to Fail

When I was suffered from extreme anxiety, my late night drinking left me exhausted the next day. To counteract the effects, I overcompensated with caffeine. To relax from the stimulants jitters and anxiety, I drank. From this vicious cycle, and without discipline, I descended into chaos. Eventually it took my "heart attack" for me to realize that anxious, drunk, and stupid was no way to go through life.

Eventually I had to stop beating myself up over these mistakes, and if you find that you are 'too hard on yourself', then you'll love the mantra I took up:

There are no losses, only lessons.

When you feel like you've failed, you need to let the past go and move forward with what you've learned so that you get better everyday.

I knew I had to cut back on these habits, so I told my friends, my family, and my email list of over 150,000 'strangers' that I was cutting back, giving up booze, and turning over a new leaf. I made a plan, shared it with the world for accountability, and changed my ways.

It was only when I had a new roadmap for life that I was able to arrive at my dream destination. This roadmap analogy is why I had you spend so much time creating your values and your vision, so that you had a plan and so that they could drive every daily decision. These provide the alignment and structure you need to become Unstoppable and dominate in business and in life. The next step in your success is to get accountability to stick to the plan.

For example, if your plan includes quitting a habit, figure out what you can do to make yourself accountable for that goal.

If you're trying to cut back on caffeine, tell everyone in the office, make sure your spouse knows at home, and even let your friendly neighborhood Starbucks barista know that you'll be in less often, and that under no circumstances is she allowed to serve you an espresso after noon. From there, it becomes easier to stick to your strategy of replacing your coffee intake with green tea or unsweetened ice tea. You can also select a cutoff time for caffeine, say noon, and tell your friends and team members that if they catch you drinking coffee after a certain time, then you owe them twenty dollars. I know, I know, sounds crazy, but accountability doesn't work without consequences.

Better planning, preparation, being accountable to someone, and replacing bad habits with good ones will make it easier to transform your misaligned lifestyle for an aligned one with less anxiety. Other strategies are useful for managing specific challenges you might discover with sticking to your plan, especially when it comes to tackling habits that create compounding stress, such as procrastination.

Bedros, who you'll hear about often in this book, and who doesn't mind me sharing these stories, provides a good example of this. Bedros used to procrastinate during his workday, putting off the hard stuff until later in the day, and eventually moving it to after dinner. He'd eat late, work on the tough stuff, and finally get to sleep around one or two in the morning. Exhausted, Bedros would sleep in and wake up behind on the next day's activities. This is how procrastination can snowball into an anxiety-filled lifestyle, where you're always playing catch-up.

One strategy for avoiding procrastination is to take care of your most difficult tasks first, or as Mark Twain put it, "Eat a live frog first thing in the morning and nothing worse will happen to you the rest of the day." Brian Tracy's book *Eat That Frog* is based on this strategy. If you have a difficult task ahead of you, do it first. Eat the frog first thing, before you do anything else. If you have two frogs to deal with, eat the biggest, ugliest one first.

Action Beats Anxiety. Motion Beats Meditation. Work Beats Worry.

In the last chapter, you planned your Perfect Day Script. Prioritizing your activities focuses on taking care of the most important tasks first, but you should also consider which tasks are the toughest—those you probably dread the most. Make those your first tasks of the day, and you'll have an early win every day. Those morning victories will change how you feel about yourself and make the rest of the day a lot easier. Or like Twain said, "nothing worse will happen to you the rest of the day."

Change Your Mindset, Change Your Life

If you're anything like me, from a blue-collar background of modest means, you've probably grown up with a set of limiting beliefs. You might have a poor money mindset, a scarcity mentality, and irrational fear of losing everything (all of which I've had to overcome). Or you might have been told early on in life that you're only capable of being so wealthy, so fit, so attractive, so successful. As you grow older, you begin to label yourself too: introvert, extrovert, creative, analytical. However, these labels make it hard for you to change, and in a way, they become self-fulfilling prophecies. Think about your labels: Are they serving your best interests? If they aren't helping you meet your values- and vision-driven goals, probably not.

For years I put myself in the "Introvert Box." Because I was naturally anxious in social settings, I began to give myself excuses for taking the easy way out, skipping meals and events with business partners, drinking excessively to take the edge off, or being rude and stand-offish when meeting new people.

At one point, early in my career before I decided to make changes, I would even request the lowest floor possible at hotels so that I could avoid being in elevators with strangers.

As I matured I realized that being labeled put in the "Introvert Box" did not serve me, and in fact, only imprisoned me in anxiety. It held me back from success and was the complete antithesis of the growth mindset I believe in for all other areas of my life. What labels are you putting on yourself that do not serve you? Where are you taking the easy way out or the path of least resistance? And how are these decisions fueling your anxiety or holding you back from achieving your goals?

These are the tough questions we must ask in periods of introspection. These are the limits we must overcome and the changes we must make. And while they might sound terrifying, or at least annoying and uncomfortable, this is the path to true freedom in your life.

Eventually, as with so many of my fatal flaws in life, I decided enough was enough and that I had to flip the script in my mind. This was essential in order to match the world's view of me (successful, smart, disciplined) with my internal beliefs. Eliminating this misalignment was important for overcoming my anxiety forever.

Ask anyone who knew me ten years ago and they'll rave about how today I'm a totally different person. They might even joke about aliens abducting me and replacing me with some new positive, enthusiastic, energetic version of the crusty old me. I no longer fear networking events, and I even talk to strangers in elevators. It makes me a little embarrassed to remember how I behaved in the past, but all that really matters is how I – and how you can – live in the present. If I can change and break out of my box, you can too. We don't have to let our old labels hold us down.

Consider the story of the baby elephant whose tamer kept him on a leash tied to a stick in the ground. No matter how hard he pulled, the little elephant couldn't dislodge the stick to free himself. Eventually, he stopped trying. The elephant grew and grew to a ten-foot-high, ten-thousand-pound beast, yet he remained leashed to that same stick in the ground, because he didn't believe he could move it. This is what happens to you when you cling to those old limiting beliefs about yourself—they keep you in one place, tied to a stick, so to speak. You can change these beliefs over time, but accountability will nudge you in the right direction, so you can begin to make that transformation more quickly.

Changing what you believe about yourself also requires a bit of mental reprogramming. It requires you to adopt a growth mindset, and believe that you are always capable of learning, that you are never stuck with whatever that image is that you have of yourself. That old image only limits your potential, but you have it within your power to create a new image and evolve into it. You can abandon your old habits and develop new ones. You can learn new skills, develop new talents, and become healthier, wealthier, and wiser at any age. Your growth doesn't stop when you graduate college, or when you hit 30, 40, 50, or even 60 years old. You can continue growing as long as you believe that you can, and with a growth mindset, you can. "The best is yet to come," Bedros always says, and so your best days are not behind you, they're ahead, and they can keep getting better as long as you continue to become more unstoppably aligned, structured, and accountable.

Abundance Beats Anxiety

Entrepreneurs often suffer from an irrational fear of losing everything they've worked so hard to attain and achieve. Unfortunately, this can create what's known as a scarcity mindset, which is not conducive to growth.

Why is this issue so prevalent in entrepreneurs and other go-getters? It may be because many of them came from a place of modest means and are terrified of ending up where they started. Many of them have a sort of chip on their shoulder and feel like they have something to prove to the world. Once they've made their first million, or ten million, or whatever, they mistakenly switch from playing offense to defense, will fight and claw to hang onto it, fearing that someone or something could take it away at any moment.

Of course, that is irrational. Barring a natural disaster, horrible accident, or really, *really* poor decision making, you're not going to lose everything, and even if you did lose your money, you'll still have your network, your skills, and your experience. Still, it's normal to reach a certain level in your career, look back at where you came from, compare that situation to where you are now, and have a tiny moment of terror, worrying that someday you might have to start from scratch.

The solution for scarcity thinking is an abundance mindset. Instead of worrying what might happen to what you have now consider everything you could possibly accomplish in your lifetime. Think BIG. What you capable of achieving with your skills, your knowledge, and your connections? The sky's the limit, right? And you're just getting started.

Will you be able to meet those goals if you're focused on protecting your assets, instead of moving forward? Playing defense precludes you from taking risks, learning, and growing. Having a vision, but being too afraid to act on it, creates anxiety. Again, seek alignment. Know what you want and go after it.

This is another reason you need to have someone in place to whom you are accountable. Without that accountability, you'll be tempted to take the path of least resistance, which is staying exactly where you are, in your little comfort zone bubble. But this is not where your BIG self needs to live. Instead, you need to step-up and step-in to your greatness. You need to continue on your hero's journey, following your path toward your goals, not sitting on the sidelines for the rest of your life.

Instead of letting fear hijack your mindset, channel it toward greater success. At one time, remember, you were not an entrepreneur. Somehow you found the energy, the time, and the motivation to bring yourself to your current level of success. Rather than allowing a scarcity mindset to hinder your progress or cause you to become complacent, use that fear as an incentive. See it for what it is, irrational, ridiculous, but understandable, too, and then move on. Continue on your path, providing even more value to your friends, family, clients, and the world.

Your A-Team For Overcoming Anxiety

In my book *The Perfect Day Formula*, I describe what I call the Five Pillars of Success, which are:

1. Planning and preparation

2. Professional accountability

3. Positive social support

4. A meaningful incentive

5. A big deadline

These pillars—especially the second and third pillar—also play a part in accountability as it supports Unstoppable Alignment and structure and reducing anxiety. The second pillar, professional accountability, refers to your coach or mentor—the person to whom who hold yourself accountable.

One of my accountability mentors is Matt Smith, my business partner at Early To Rise. Matt was a huge help in getting me to change my ways from crusty old Craig to the man I've become today. Matt would often sternly, but kindly call me out on my interactions with people. He told my bluntly when I was acting inappropriately. He told me he knew I could do better, and set a higher standard for me in many areas of my life. Because I trusted and respected Matt, and because I looked up to him as a big brother and didn't want to disappoint him, I made a serious effort to change my ways. It worked, and I was able to overcome many aspects of my social anxiety and my limiting self-beliefs and evolve into the coach, speaker, and author that the world needed me to be.

When you're seeking someone to be accountable to, choose wisely. Select a person who know you well, knows what you're capable of, and has your best interests at heart. It must be someone that sees the greatness inside of you, and who sincerely wants you to step into it. But it also must be someone willing to have difficult conversations with you, as Matt did with me, and call you out if you don't live up to their standards. Accountability is ineffective without significant consequences, and there must be nothing worse than disappointing this person. When you have that factor in place, you can overcome the anxiety in the way and move mountains in your life

The third pillar, positive social support, represents the people with whom you surround yourself. Once you have an accountability coach or mentor, build a network of positive people who have achieved what you want to achieve and who will support you on your hero's journey. If you surround yourself with people who don't share your vision, you'll be tempted to engage in behaviors and activities that pull you away from where you want to be. You know what that will do to your anxiety, right?

This doesn't mean you have to abandon your old friends, but you should control your activities with those who tend to pull you away from your goals. Like Bedros, you might have to block a few people or environments from your life, and I'll show you how to do this in a kind and respectful manner in later chapters. But for now just understand that if your social circle includes people that take you down a slippery slope of anxiety-inducing behaviors, then something's gotta give, and we can't let it be your goals and dreams.

You cannot hang out with negative people and expect to live a positive life. Peer pressure is often the toughest test of your commitment. If you want to succeed, stay strong and do what is right for you.

Years ago I was given this great advice from an incredible speaker and entrepreneur, Nido Qubein. It's a little exercise I still revisit from time to time.

"Make a list of the 10 people you spend the most time with and your top 5 goals and top 5 values," Nido said. "Compare the lists. Are the people you spend the most time with congruent with your values and goals? If not, you might be held back by this association."

When you spend time with others who have the same goals as you, and who are making progress towards these goals, that you too will have greater success.

To help you attract the right people and positive support into your social network, here is the **Ultimate Guide to Finding Good People in Your Life**

Step 1) Identify what you value in people.

Step 2) Identify where this type of person spends time.

Step 3) Go there.

Whether it is a church, gym, beach, dance lessons, a fitness class, Chamber of Commerce meeting, local lectures, weekend seminar, or a positive Facebook forum, there are good people out there. For instance, if you want to be a successful entrepreneur, you need to grow your circle of influence, and you aren't going to do that sitting at home on your couch. You need to be out attending my workshops, joining Masterminds, and getting connect with people who "been there and done that" when it comes to your big goals and dreams.

Take full responsibility for your social network, just as you take responsibility for your results in all areas of life. If what you are doing now is not working, then you must change. Don't rely on doing "normal" things to get extraordinary results, because it doesn't work that way. Normal and average behaviors only get you average results, and those just aren't very good these days.

When I was on my hero's journey and changing my old ways, I was careful to surround myself with people who had the characteristics and success that I wished to achieve. I sought out positive people with great energy, who didn't gossip, wanted only the best for others, and who were incredibly generous with their time, money, and energy. That led me to spending more time with Bedros, Matt, Jason Ferruggia, and my friend Joel Marion (the most generous person I have ever met). They served as role models and challenged me to work through my social anxiety, come out of my shell, and step into my greatness. It wasn't easy, and there might be times you resist your mentors advice and encouragement, as I often did. I wanted to push back, to take the easy way out, but I didn't, and you won't either.

This decision, to be around people who encourage and support your dreams, your values, and your vision, will change your life more than any other advice I can give you.

Making a Big Leap For a Better Life

Accountability isn't a one-time fix for your anxiety. It's a lifestyle change that demands ongoing, deliberate attention. Though I've reined in my bad habits and developed behaviors that align with my goals, I continue to evolve with a growth mindset that encourages learning, improvement, and more alignment. Just because I proved to myself that I can go for X number of years without drinking or swearing doesn't mean I should allow myself to lapse for a day. Rather, I'm aware of where I am and the work it took to get here, and I know that if I continue on this path, the sky's the limit.

It's the same for you. The choices you make and actions you take either move you closer to or further from your goals. If you've restricted your social media time to 20 minutes a day, stick to it. You may think that checking it one more time during the day will relieve some stress, but it won't, because you know that's not in line with your goals. Acting against your goals is what brings on the anxiety. In essence, short-term relief actually leads to long-term pain, whereas short-term pain (resisting the urge to check social media) leads to long-term gain—and victory.

I mentioned at the beginning of this chapter that public accountability is an incredible motivator. This is one place where social media can actually help you. Announce your goals to all your friends on social media. "I'm quitting smoking." "I'm going to do a dozen presentations this year." "I'm writing a book." I even encouraged one client, Zander Fryer, to announce that he was going to find the love of his life in 90 days or less. The skeptics had their say, of course, but sure enough, by making this commitment and being held accountable (by me and others), he accomplished his goal with days to spare. Imagine that. Imagine what stepping up and stepping into your greatness, sharing your big dreams and declaring your intentions to the world could change in your life. When you make this decision you'll attract more positive people into your life, and this virtuous circle will accelerate your results and help you move further away from stress and anxiety.

Major Key To All of This: Identifying What's Important

When you have many big goal and dreams, there is a serious risk of getting overwhelmed with opportunity. That's why I want to teach you another very important planning practice that will set you free from anxiety and put you on the path to faster success.

Many people spend their time focusing on what's urgent. But if you spend your entire life putting out fires and dealing with other people's emergencies, you'll never achieve your goals. For example, I hear from people all the time that tell me they want to write a book. I then see that person six months later, ask them how the book is going, and hear this tired old refrain, "I just can't find the time to start."

The problem is that you can't "find time." It's not like time is hidden under the bed collecting dust with your old Ab Rocker machine. You don't find time for what matters, you must MAKE time for what matters.

So many of these potential book authors start the day with email, phone calls, replying to comments on social media, and responding to every seemingly urgent request from other people. They are too busy in activity to ever accomplish anything. This constant reactive mode prevents so man people from moving forward on what matters. You see, if you leave the most important things to the end of day, you will never do them. You'll take care of the urgent tasks, but you'll always neglect the critical tasks, the goals that will make the greatest difference in your life.

"One day you will wake up and there won't be any more time to do the things you've always wanted," the author Paulo Coelho warns. "Do it now."

This story about one of my future author friends actually had a happy ending. I worked with him to set a deadline for writing the book. Then, we rescheduled his reactive work, like answering email, to later in the day and prioritized writing his book, moving that to the early hours of the morning when he had more energy and discipline to accomplish the task. Use this strategy on your own career. If you're using the most productive time of your day to react, respond, or do busywork, stop it. Schedule the big stuff—writing that book, developing a new product, or crafting that sales presentation—for the high-energy part of your day. Set a time and a deadline and get it done.

In three years' time, you will not remember all those emails or text messages that seemed so urgent. But you will remember the big goals you achieved the aligned with your values, visions, and your dreams..

The Paradox of Pushing

Finally, becoming accountable means testing your own boundaries, stepping out of your comfort zone, and pushing your limits. That sounds anxiety-inducing, right? But this is another paradox of anxiety: the more you cling to that comfort zone, the longer you'll be hindered by anxiety. Pulling yourself out of that zone is what ultimately allows you to create an anxiety-free, Unstoppable life.

Flip the script inside your head, the one that says "anxious." Whenever you're feeling anxious, tell yourself that it's excitement. Feeling fearful? That's anticipation, because you're about to do something great. Are you overwhelmed? You are about to experience a major breakthrough. All these things will lead you toward a life of less anxiety, so go with them. Embrace them, embrace life.

Exercise: 90-Day Blueprint

Commit to accomplishing one big goal in the next 90 days. When you focus on one project, it helps you say 'no' to taking on too much, stops you from feeling overwhelmed, and reduces your anxiety. Focus also gives you clarity and structure, further reducing your stress. In this exercise choose one major work project to complete, a skill to master, or some kind of transformation that aligns with your values and vision. Then complete the following worksheet. Identify a numbers-based outcome goal and three process goals (action steps) that will help you reach that goal. The difference between an outcome goal and a process goal is that while you don't fully control the achievement of the outcome goal, you do have full control over the process goals (that is you have full control over your ability to take action). You can use this planner for both personal and professional goals, but pick a project that will go the furthest in reducing your anxiety levels right now.

Here's a simple example of how to complete this exercise. Let's say Mrs. Jones came to me and said, "Craig, I want to lose 20 pounds in the next 90 days." Great, that's her outcome goal. We'd then identify the three most important action steps to achieve this goal. Those steps would be going to Fit Body Boot Camp three times per week, following a whole-foods diet 90% of the time (with room for one cheat meal on the weekend), and drinking three liters of water per day. If Mrs. Jones followed through on all three of those process goals for the next 90 days, she'd get as close to her outcome goal as possible. Next, we can break down those big action steps into smaller goals and quick victories. We'd identify what she can do in the next 24 hours (such as signing up for Fit Body Boot Camp and tossing all the junk food in her house), 72 hours (such as going to her first workout and buying a water bottle to carry with her at work), 7 days (reporting to an accountability buddy), 14 days (checking in with a nutritionist to help her through any meal planning problems), 21 days (recruiting a friend to be a supportive workout buddy), and 30 days (reviewing her progress to see what's working and where she still needs extra help).

Here's one more example that will connect with entrepreneurs. Let's say Mrs. Smith comes to me and says, "Craig, I want to get 100 new customers in the next 90 days." Great, that's her outcome goal. The three process goals might be to implement a referral strategy, run a new 30-day challenge using Facebook ads to generate leads, and train a new salesperson to do in-person consults. Next, we'd plan out the next thirty days. In 24 hours she could hire write referral scripts for her team members to use when interacting with current clients and post a job ad for the new sales person. In 72 hours she could hold a team meeting teaching the proper use of the scripts, and she could create a Facebook ad for the 30-day challenge. In the next 7 days Mrs. Smith would have started generating leads with the Facebook ads and reviewed the resumes for the new sales position. In 14 days she and her team would have launched the challenge and interviewed salesperson candidates. In 21 days Mrs. Smith will have made the final decision on the new salesperson and done a review meeting of the referral strategy implementation. And finally, after 30 days, she would have trained the new salesperson and set up sales consults with the referrals and new 30-day challenge leads. If Mrs. Smith continues on this pace, she'll do everything she possibly can to get those 100 new clients in 90 days.

You can see how the power of clarity and focus from this one simple exercise will dramatically reduce the feeling of being overwhelmed, stressed, or anxious. Your next steps become clear when the path to success is laid out before you. Now it's time for you to create your 90-Day plan.

90-Day Outcome Goal

_____

_____

- Process Goal #1

_____

_____

- Process Goal #2

_____

_____

- Process Goal #3

_____

_____

  o 24-Hour To Do

_____

_____

  o 72-Hour To-Do

_____

_____

  o 7-Day To-Do

_____

_____

  o 14-Day To Do

_____

_____

  o 21-Day To-Do

_____

_____

  o 30-Day To-Do

_____

_____

Summary

- Everyone is raised with certain limiting beliefs, but becoming Unstoppable requires you to become accountable for your choices, behaviors, and actions.

- Identifying a mentor or coach to hold you accountable, and find your support network, are the biggest decisions that can move you ahead to your big goals and dreams

- Building a blueprint for focusing on your big goal in the next 90 days can move mountains in your life because it reduces anxiety and gives your clarity.

MASTERING UNSTOPPABLE HABITS

―――

Part Two of becoming Unstoppable is about taking care of you. I know what you're thinking: "Craig, I don't have time for exercise or meditation, let alone getting a massage." I understand, but if you don't take care of yourself now, one day you're going to wake up with a very expensive bill to pay. The day you experience having your physical or mental well-being stolen from you is the day you'll finally understand what people mean when they say that health is everything. That said, it's my job to make sure that doesn't happen to you. And so the next section of this book is dedicated to showing you simple and effective ways to fight off, and even reverse anxiety.

You need to take care of yourself and overcome your anxiety first, before you can bring your best self to your work, your relationships, and the world. As cliché as it is, there's no better analogy than what you've heard in every flight safety video where they say, "Please put your oxygen mask on first before assisting others." You must take care of your mental and physical health if you want to be your best self, serve others, and overcome anxiety.

Building unstoppable habits is the fastest way to experience a noticeable reduction in your anxiety levels. In this section, you'll learn a one-minute breathing technique that can lift the weight of the world from your shoulders, and I'll show you certain foods you need to avoid eating, and how even the busiest high-performer can fit in regular stints of anxiety-fighting (and fun) exercise. Exercise is one of the most scientifically proven ways to reduce stress, and we'll give you an easy-to-follow plan in Chapter Four, *Nutrition and Exercise*.

In Chapter Five, *Breathing and Sleep*, you'll learn how small changes in the way you inhale and exhale can help you relax, and you'll get some of my hacks so you can get more sleep, so that ultimately you'll have less stress and anxiety. I've already mentioned how breathing the wrong way contributed to my anxiety, and most people don't know how to breathe in a way that calms the body down, or how our bad postural habits can make our days more stressful. Sleep is also underrated—and underutilized—in our modern society to help in fighting anxiety and improving overall health, and we'll discuss how to use a very simple system to fall asleep faster, sleep more deeply, and wake up with more energy and less anxiety.

In Chapter Six, we'll explore *Yoga and Meditation*. Don't roll your eyes— gone are the days where there was a negative stigma around practicing yoga and meditation. Today both are used by some of the world's richest and most successful people (Ray Dalio, Tony Robbins, Sara Blakely, almost every Hollywood actor, most professional athletes, and my most successful clients). You'll discover how just a few minutes of daily yoga and/or meditation can unlock immediate and lasting benefits for reducing anxiety and I'll explain why yoga and meditation are so valuable that even a guy like me—a former bodybuilding, bro-type jock—won't go one day without them.

CHAPTER 4

THE ANXIETY DIET

"Let food be thine medicine"

– HIPPOCRATES

In the summer of 2013, when Bedros Keuilian suffered a massive anxiety attack, he had all the mental triggers: overworked, stressed at work, and suffering in silence. But he had a lot of physical triggers pushing his anxiety button too. He would work late and struggle to get up in the morning. Tired, he would fuel himself with caffeine. His exercise habits were inconsistent. And he'd end almost every evening – and sometimes in the middle of the night – "standing at the kitchen counter stress eating 2,000 to 3,000 calories of comfort food carbs and fat like bread, peanut butter, pretzels, and cream cheese, all washed down with a soda. And then after self-medicating with food, I'd go back to sleep. Then I'd wake up in the morning hating myself, which only caused even more anxiety."

His diet didn't cause anxiety, but it certainly didn't help. After his wake-up call, Bedros realized he had to Man-Up. He became a better leader at work, he opened up and began communicating better with his family, he began seeing a therapist to talk out his problems, and to be frank, he finally began implementing the structure, routine, and habits that he learned from me. He goes to bed and gets up at the same time every day. He limits his caffeine intake to one iced coffee from Starbucks before 10 o'clock in the morning. He exercises six days per week.

Today, Bedros is anxiety free, no longer suffers in silence, in the best physical condition of his life, his business is growing faster than ever, he has more time for his family, not less, and his diet and exercise regimens are a key to his success. He eats several small meals per day, doesn't binge, has cut the junk food, and has control over his habits, rather than letting his old bad habits control him.

One of my teachers had a saying: Food is as powerful as drugs.

It's scientifically proven. What you put in your body causes measureable physiological effects that can quickly change how well you feel and perform. If you consume a lot of alcohol or sugar, for example, you increase the inflammation in your body. That leads to poor health and low energy, which then leads to stress, and stress leads to anxiety.

One of the best examples of food acting like a drug is coffee, mostly because coffee contains the most popular drug in the world, caffeine. The problem is that many people become anxious when they have too much caffeine. Caffeine, like most stimulants, elevates levels of adrenaline in your blood stream—which increase stress and anxiety. I've found that if you are sensitive to caffeine and have more than 100 mg of caffeine (less than the amount in most coffees or in a can of Monster energy drinks), you have a much greater risk for anxiety over the course of the day. Some people are even more sensitive, and even the slightest bit of caffeine can cause them to feel overwhelmed and anxious.

A trip to Starbucks is like adding rocket fuel to anxiety. Even a decaf coffee delivers 25 mg of caffeine, half of that in a can of Coke. A Grande Americano clocks in at 225 mg, the equivalent of nearly three Red Bulls (don't tell the nurse!). Your beloved Pumpkin Spice Latte? It hits you with 75mg to 150mg of anxiety-inducing, sleep-disturbing caffeine. Even a Grande Green Tea contains 80 mg (one small can of Red Bull!). That's why my Starbucks drink of choice has become, much to my friends' amusement, a Grande Mint Majesty (0 mg of caffeine, all while delivering the scent of peppermint which has been show to increase alertness).

It's not easy kicking a coffee or caffeine habit—it can even be physically painful to abandon it. If you give up caffeine cold turkey—dropping from three hundred milligrams per day to nothing, for instance—you'll likely suffer from withdrawal headaches and other symptoms. However, in the long run, your anxiety will be much better off if you reduce your daily caffeine intake. Start with switching one of your coffees to Green Tea or decaf, and then eventually join me on the Mint Majesty train.

Of course you will not "cure" anxiety by simply reducing or eliminating sugar, caffeine, and alcohol, but you will move in the right direction. Anxiety is a powerful force, and there's no magical food or diet to eliminate it. However, if you eat to support your unstoppable habits—whole, natural foods, lots of fruits and vegetables, nuts, healthy fats, healthy protein sources—and drink lots of water, you'll be on the right path. And while you don't have to give up caffeine and alcohol entirely, you'll want to keep them to a minimum as you embrace the other anti-anxiety strategies detailed in this book.

Abs Don't Beat Anxiety

When I had my anxiety attacks I was 185 pounds, 9% body fat, had six-pack abs, could bench press over 275 pounds and run a sub 6-minute mile. But being fit doesn't mean squat when anxiety has your number. On the other hand, being unable to climb three flights of stairs doesn't do you any good either.

When it comes to exercise for anxiety, there is no best approach. It's not like I'd be able to design you an anti-anxiety workout, as I did for millions of people during my career as a fat loss guru.

Instead, I'd even warn you about overdoing your exercise intensity around periods of anxiety. Too much exercise causes physical stress that your overactive mind might interpret as feelings of anxiety. That can play tricks on you, get your mind racing and anxiety engine revving, and leave you worse off than you started.

What matters the most for first managing, and then attacking anxiety is that you build a strong habit of consistent exercise. Building in an exercise routine helps you to take back control of a life might seem like it is spiraling out of control.

You need to use exercise (and diet) as the foundation of your recovery. Exercise can help you learn to breathe better (through yoga, Tai Chi, qigong, etc.). Exercise can support your return to social settings through group classes and positive interactions at the gym. An exercise routine can also get you outside, in the sunshine, as my daily walk with Bally the Dog always "forced" upon me.

Most important, an exercise program provides the critical routine and rituals that your mind and body crave each day. Whether you are traveling or at home, sticking to daily movement is essential for your physical and mental health. Don't worry about becoming the next extreme athlete or American Ninja Warrior. Instead seek out the exercise regimen that serves your recovery and relief. We can always build up from there once your body and brain are back to normal.

When you're suffering through anxiety, exercise might feel like the last thing you want to do, but it is one of the most beneficial things you can do. Due to the chemicals released and neurotransmitters activated by exercise, you feel better when you do it—especially if you're able to exercise outdoors on a sunny day. A thirty-minute walk is fine. You simply want to move and be active, which will lead to better health and less anxiety.

When I went through my special kind of hell in 2006, exercise and nutrition were key components of my recovery. Even though it was difficult for me to train hard, I was still consistent in going to the gym, and taking my little puppy on daily walks to the park. Likewise, I wasn't perfect with my nutrition as I mentioned earlier, but 80 percent of my diet fit the description above, and I eliminated caffeine and alcohol during my six-week heart attack. Diet and exercise were important for my physical and mental health and will be the same for you.

While on our roads to recovery, both Bedros and I discovered an important, but vital lesson about the human body. We are wired for routine. Our body rewards us when we go to bed, wake up, eat, exercise, work, and rest on the same schedule everyday. You've likely recognized this at a slow point in your life, perhaps in September when you get back on track after the summer holidays and are eating at home most nights. Suddenly you're sleeping better, have more all-day energy, feel less stressed, and get more done. That's your body – and mind – thanking you for being in a routine.

Unfortunately, high performers don't get to enjoy a simple schedule for long. Maybe your work is seasonal, like my father's on the farm, where there were long days during the sowing and harvest seasons, putting his schedule out of place. Or maybe, like me, you travel a lot, bouncing between time zones like a pinball, wondering when you wake up: Where am I, what day is it, and who moved the bathroom overnight?

Some people let their routines go off the rails when they travel. I've traveled with many professionals who think that as soon as you step into an airport that it's license to eat like you're at an-inclusive resort in Mexico. But defaulting to bad habit triggers is a breeding ground for anxiety. That's why, even when you are a road warrior (well, especially when you are a road warrior), you must stick to diet and exercise recommendations in this section. When you create consistent habits around diet and exercise, your body is able to give your brain the support it needed to return to normal, and eventually become the unstoppable high performer you need to be to grow your business.

What you eat and if you are exercise are factors that lie completely within your control. These are changes you can start right away, and that you can build upon for more lasting results and relief from anxiety, because they begin a virtuous cycle that lead to more positive habits. When you exercise regularly and eat healthy, you'll get a better night's sleep and avoid adding any unnecessary stress to your brain or body. Day by day, walk by walk, meal by meal, you'll start to feel better, more in control, and on the road to recovery.

Make the Connection Through Introspection

Self-reflection is one of the best tools for helping you fix problems in life. It allows us to identify "cause and effect," and make connections between our behaviors and our results. For example, if you toss and turn in bed at night, a little introspection will help you realize that the 4 p.m. trip to Starbucks for the Venti Americano was the culprit. When you do this self-reflection daily, you can identify good decisions and bad behaviors, and going forward you can then do more of what works and less of what doesn't. Most of us learned this phenomenon the hard way when we were kids. Put your hand on the stove and you'll feel a lot of pain. Therefore, never put your hand on the stove again!

Through introspection, we can find ways to escape from anxiety. I recognized that drinking too much alcohol left me with a burning sensation over my heart the next day. It was the warning sign that anxiety was about to attack. Over time, I reduced my alcohol intake to nearly nothing and likewise, eliminated my risk of suffering from a full-blown attack.

I want you to put on your Sherlock Holmes hat (because I just know you have one lying around the house), sit back, and apply the same cause-and-effect investigation to your life. Does caffeine make you anxious? Does that glass of wine at night calm you down in the short term but interfere with your sleep at night so you wake up anxious in the a.m.? Does exercising outside make you feel better than going to the gym? There is a lot of experimentation that goes on when you're trying to understand and reduce your anxiety, so just begin with easy ones. Try a greens drink instead of a Grande Americano in the afternoon, or do deep breathing instead of a deep dive into social media when you have "5 minutes to kill.' Observe how you feel before, during, and after these small shifts in your behavior. You'll start to see how small actions can lead to big results when it comes to reducing anxiety and sparking positive changes, and then you can build on the better ones as you do more of what works and less of what doesn't.

One of the differences between anxiety and depression is that most anxiety comes on in response to a physical or mental trigger. That's why it is *critically* important to identify the triggers of your anxiety. For me, it was weekend binge-drinking with certain friends that knew no limits, compensating with too much caffeine, waking up late and checking email first thing, and letting my to-do list pile up until it seemed overwhelming and impossible to overcome. What are the triggers for you? Maybe you get stressed out from interactions with certain negative people, or maybe your nightly binge-watching of television shows is getting out of hand, leaving your mind racing and preventing you from getting enough sleep. Perhaps your obsession with the hapless New York Jets is consuming your energy, wasting your time, and elevating your anxiety. Or maybe your nutrition was perfect all week long, but when the weekend came along, you ate cheat meals loaded with junk food, consumed too much alcohol, and sacrificed your sleep. Then, the next thing you knew, an anxiety attack was knocking on your door. These are the cause-and-effect connections you need to identify and when your sleuthing identifies them, you must eliminate those triggers from your life to take a massive step toward reducing your anxiety levels and kicking it to the curb for good.

For instance, if you're like most people, you probably know how much caffeine it takes to make you anxious. I'm not saying it's easy to avoid caffeine, especially when you're exhausted at 3 p.m. and you have a work project that is likely going to take you to 7 p.m., but it's important to at least know your limits (and your options, like the ones listed above). Once you do, you can start working on strategies to avoid going beyond. Most people also know how they feel the morning after drinking too much alcohol. Again, it's easy to know your limits, but a lot harder to stick to them if you're out on a business dinner with three extroverted salesmen that love to "tie one on." That said, if excessive caffeine and alcohol are your triggers, then you need to design your life to avoid these environments, control your intake, and keep yourself out of trouble.

Fortunately, it's not as impossible as you think. You need to reevaluate your personal behaviors to keep yourself away from trouble. Observe your actions and your habits. Do you reach for coffee, alcohol, or soda because they are convenient, or because you've never thought about putting boundaries around consumption? You might have to remove the soda and alcohol from your house. You might have to tell your coach, as many of my clients say to me, that you are no longer drinking alcohol during the week (aka "on school nights") so that you can be more alert and focused every morning. You might have to promise an accountability buddy that you won't drink coffee after lunch and that if you do, then you owe them ten bucks. Anxiety is an extreme condition, and extreme actions are required to attack it.

When it comes to improving your habits, your early wins snowball into bigger victories. People joining exercise programs are a great example of this. One day they find a great trainer, have an amazing workout, and feel energized all day. They feel so fantastic from the endorphin rush that they commit to even more exercise, better nutrition, and cutting back on vices. The next morning, they might think, "Wow, I didn't eat crappy food last night, and I didn't drink three glasses of wine, I slept like a champ, and I felt awesome when I woke up today. Let's do it again!" Soon they've lost ten pounds, twenty pounds or more, and reversed decades of decadence.

This is also why it is so important to start your day right. Waking up on time, doing a little bit of exercise, and eating healthy food in the morning gives you a victory—and this victory gives you progress, momentum, and motivation to stick to better decisions for the rest of the day. When lunchtime comes around, you're much more likely to think, "I'm doing so well today that I want to make sure I eat well at lunch, and I'm not going to ruin it later by drinking a bottle of wine at night." This daisy chain reaction of positive choices is a small, but significant step in reducing stress and increasing success.

Once you start to feel better, you'll want to do more of what works, and less of what doesn't work. This requires you to stick to your daily habit of self-reflection. Take notice if anxiety surfaces when you have a large morning coffee instead of a smoothie and make the connection between a mid-day walk in the sun and how you feel calm in the afternoon. Once you begin to find the right way to live, you can then continue to make the right decisions to keep anxiety at bay.

An Alcoholic's Guide to Getting Back on Track When You Go Off the Rails

We all want to be free from anxiety, but I can hear you now saying, "Sounds great, Craig, but there's no way my life is going to include eight hours of sleep, yoga, and a green smoothie every morning. Remember—I'm a hard-charging entrepreneur with kids, a mortgage, and deadlines."

I understand, and let's be real, you'll often find yourself in situations where you won't have healthy options or be surrounded with supportive people. That's okay—everybody stumbles. If you get off track, don't add to the anxiety and beat yourself up. Being excessively hard on yourself does not serve you. You can minimize mistakes by planning and preparing, but the important thing is to get back on track as quickly as possible.

During my binge-drinking alcoholic days, I'd often join my friends in overeating pizza at 3 in the morning, or worse, stumble home late at night and gorge on my vice, chocolate covered almonds (but hey, they were "dark chocolate," healthy-fat almonds!). The next morning, I'd be hungover AND bloated, uncomfortable both physically and mentally. If I let myself worry about it, engage in negative self-talk, or mope, things only got worse. Instead, I took the attitude that every step, every second, and every action took me further from the mistake and closer to redemption. I focused on controlling the now, not regretting the past. In fact, I even chose to spend time in helpful self-reflection, identifying the triggers that got me into trouble, so I could avoid them in the future. It was these victories of turning adversity into advantage that allowed me to eventually overcome these challenges, and now, when placed in the wrong environment, even under pressure, I'm able to perform in a way that's best for my health and my right life.

Action Beats Anxiety. Motion Beats Meditation. Work Beats Worry.

When bad things happen to good people (i.e. you), forgive yourself for the mistakes of the past, learn your lessons, and move on. Your short-term focus should be on getting back to healthy habits fast, so you'll quickly feel the benefits and achieve small victories that can be built upon further. This will create a snowball of success, and away you go, back on track to getting better every day—and further away from anxiety and its triggers. Your ultimate goal is to make your healthy habits automatic, so that when you don't do them, you immediately recognize it, understand that it's minor damage that can be dealt with, and then focus on getting back on track as fast as possible.

Plan Your Work and Work Your Plan

Most people struggle to change diet and exercise. Even though I've spent thousands of hours exercising in gyms, if I walked into a new gym without a workout plan for the day, I'd be just as lost as you, wandering around without an exact idea of what to do. In most cases the end result would be a bad workout and a sense of frustration and wasted time.

Planning is the key.

In their book, *Switch: How to Change Things When Change is Hard*, Chip and Dan Heath use the analogy that when you're trying to change your habits, you're like a person riding an elephant down a path. To make the ride as smooth as possible, the first thing you need to do is to get rid of all the tree branches (obstacles) in the way.

Similarly, if want to create the habit of exercising in the morning, you need to put your workout clothes beside your bed. That way, you can't use the "I don't know what to wear to my workout" excuse in the morning. Whatever your new habit, you need to overcome the obstacles that get in the way of making the right decisions. The goal of removing obstacles, eliminating temptations, and destroying distractions around good habits is to make the new behaviors easy and automatic and eliminate the need for discipline and willpower. When you do that, you make life less stressful and you become more successful. It's that simple, and over time you build a powerful set of habits that leave you unstoppable.

How to Roll the Snowball of Success

Your new habits have a broader impact on everything you do and create a chain reaction of behavior and larger habits. If you wake up late and dash over to Dunkin' Donuts for a giant coffee with two creams and two sugars, what will the rest of your day look like?

First of all, you've wreaked havoc on your blood sugar levels, paving the way for other bad and impulsive choices as the day goes on. The next thing you know you're thinking, "Well,

I've already done this, so I might as well snort that line of cocaine." (Since people automatically go from Dunkin' Donuts to cocaine, as you know!) My point is that if you make one bad decision, you will likely let yourself off the hook and start giving yourself permission to make more bad decisions. If you make the right decision, however, then a positive wave of self-encouragement kicks in. "You know what, I'm on a roll here," you might tell yourself.

Imagine if you have a snowball at the top of the hill. You can either roll it down one side, which we'll call the positive slope, where the snowball grows bigger and emboldened with healthy habits. The other is the negative slope, where the snowball gets meaner, nastier, and uglier with bad habits like too much caffeine, drinking, and even drugs. Guess where you'll find anxiety waiting for you at the bottom the hill? That's why every small decision about your health, especially those made early in the day, matter so much. Knock down the right domino, and you'll feel great. But knock down a negative one, and you'll pay the price all day.

The "Un-Guru" Guide to Diet and Exercise

This is not the book where you're going to hear about 31 different types of gluten-free, paleo, and keto diets. If that's what you're looking for, I'm sorry, but I'm not your guru.

To me, a healthy, anti-anxiety diet is simple, and consists of whole, natural foods. Feel free to read this next paragraph in your mother's voice. "Eat your vegetables. Have an apple a day. No you can't have Oreos for dinner."

Personally I like author and real-food advocate Michael Pollan's 7-word diet. It goes like this, "Eat food. Not too much. Mostly plants." To that I'd add avoid processed foods from a bag or a box. I'd also tell you to cut back on caffeine and alcohol, but that's a no-brainer. Ultimately you'll have to experiment to figure out which foods work best to reduce your anxiety, but you can't go wrong eating more fruits, vegetables, nuts (like raw almonds and walnuts), and healthy protein sources.

Back in my days writing for Men's Health magazine and running fitness transformation contests, I'd often recommend keeping a food journal for clients that struggled to lose weight. Writing down everything you eat is not only a good strategy for weight loss, but this dietary introspection also allows you to spot the cause-and-effect connections between what you eat and your anxiety levels. Try keeping track of everything you eat for seven days in a row. You might be surprised by how much caffeine or sugar you consume, or you might realize that you have much less anxiety when you have more home-cooked meals. Healthy eating helps, but healthy eating alone will not cure anxiety. Likewise, exercise is beneficial, but it's not the complete solution. You're not going to exercise your way out of anxiety, but if you don't exercise at all now, just start with a daily 20-minute walk. Going for a walk amid nature is universally accepted as one of the most beneficial things you can do for your mind and body. Many a successful figure in history, from Charles Darwin to Charles Dickens, have solved problems and created masterpieces while out walking. What matters most when it comes to diet and exercise is that you are consistent and giving your body the rituals and routines it desires.

Living Your Anxiety-Free Lifestyle

I self-care solutions we've now discussed: healthy eating, cutting back on caffeine and alcohol, and being consistent with moderate exercise are cornerstones in keeping anxiety at a distance. When I found myself in the emergency room, fearing I was having a heart attack, it was because those things were out of balance in my life, and I was living at the extremes. I drank too much and partied too much. I physically exhausted my body. Eventually I woke up with an anxiety attack that wouldn't go away. When I got back to basics, and when I began to adopt other healthy habits like breathing and meditation, which we'll talk about in the next chapter, I put myself on the road to recovery, and gave my mind the space it needed to take full advantage of the unstoppable systems we created in section one of this book.

Once you understand the drug-like power of diet and exercise, your new healthy habits and lifestyle changes will be easier to begin, maintain, and build upon, toward a more successful and less stressful anxiety-free life.

Exercise: Track And Test Your Way to Safety

When I was a personal trainer, I was shocked that most of clients couldn't put "two and two together" when it came to what they ate and how they felt. Of course, who am I to talk? I kept on drinking despite the pain I knew it would bring. Fortunately, you don't have to go through the same hell I did. When you start tracking your nutrition, exercise, and lifestyle habits, you'll be able to establish 'cause-and-effect' between your behaviors and your battles. Compare what happens when you try to exist on coffee and donuts against a green smoothie and a green tea. Tracking these daily tests will help you do more of what works, and less of what doesn't, so you set yourself up for more success and less stress.

Summary

- Keep a food journal. Write down what you eat, why you eat it (hungry? tired? bored?), and how you feel after. Doing this for just a few days provides a lifetime of education on how you should eat for your best life.

- Experiment with exercise. If you're doing nothing now, start with a 20-minute walk each day. If you're already walking, add in a small amount of strength training. Track how you feel before, during, and after. Push it when appropriate, don't force any extremes.

- Eliminate lifestyle anxiety triggers. Once you see trouble from a specific test, get help to eliminate the stress. There's nothing to be gained trying to figure it out yourself. You'll get faster results when you get help from a pro.

CHAPTER 5

THE TYPE A'S GUIDE TO CALMING DOWN AND CHILLING OUT

"When you own your breath, nobody can steal your peace."

– AUTHOR UNKNOWN

Breathing is like the Rodney Dangerfield of bodily functions, it don't get no respect. Most of the time we forget we are even doing it, and it isn't a big deal, until it is. Remember back to when you were a kid and you had "your breath knocked out of you on the playground." Or think back to that time you found yourself at elevation, gasping for air. Or that time you did the most insane workout that left your lungs on fire.

It's easy to understand why breathing is overlooked in our battle against anxiety. How could something so natural and automatic be both the cause of—and solution to—the crippling effects of anxiety? People rarely think about breathing until they find out they are doing it all wrong, which is what happened to me.

The truth is this: breathing is *critically* important in reducing anxiety, and we *do* have control over our breathing. There actually *is* a proper and healthy way to breathe to attack your anxiety and leave you stress-free.

Do You Even Breathe, Bro?

Today, thanks to the increased interest in yoga and meditation, breathing is starting to get more attention about its powerful drug-like effects, just like food. Even the "bro's" of the world are embracing their inner Namaste. And for good reason, you can calm down quickly (or conversely, become anxious immediately) simply by varying the speed and technique with which you breathe.

The sequence to calm you down is simple: inhale slowly through your nose, fill up your belly with air, and then slowly exhale. Slow breathing can calm you down quickly—in as little as one minute—because it slows your sympathetic nervous system (your stress response) and activates your parasympathetic nervous system (the one in control of calming you down). This, in turn, reduces your anxiety and stress.

The problem is that throughout the day, most people breathe by taking short, shallow breaths in their upper chest. But that's the kind of breathing that leads to stress and anxiety.

In Eastern society, where yoga and meditation are commonplace, people have a positive relationship with their breathing, and a better understanding of its impact on mental and physical health. In Western society, however, we are not taught about proper and healthy breathing, and most people don't even think about it. If something was wrong with you, breathing would likely be the last place you'd look to as the cause. Yet, proper breathing can be one of the fastest, easiest, and most effective self-care tools. In overcoming your anxiety, breathing is just as important as exercise and nutrition.

Sit-Up & Chill

The scientific bridge between breathing and anxiety is adrenaline. Adrenaline—also known as epinephrine—is the neurotransmitter that causes our fight-or-flight response. If you're being chased, you want adrenaline because it heightens your sense of alertness. That's the protective side of the "fight or flight" syndrome induced by adrenaline.

Short, shallow breaths from the upper chest, the kind common amongst someone hunched over a computer or steering wheel, resemble a moderate form of hyperventilation, causing carbon dioxide (CO_2) levels to drop in the blood. Decreased CO_2 kicks the body into fight-or-flight mode, and adrenaline is pumped into the blood.

This is great if you want to fight off fatigue and stay awake, increase your alertness for a workout, or step into the octagon for an MMA fight. If you want to calm down, however, adrenaline is the *worst* possible hormone to have running through your veins.

That's why breathing is such a vital, but often ignored component of fighting off anxiety so that you can stay calm and perform at high levels all day.

Breathing was a huge problem for me, and while it's something I work on every day, due to my Type-A, high-pressure nature, I still catch myself taking short, shallow breaths, or even holding my breath in tense situations (like the day before a book deadline).

During my journey through anxiety hell, I had no idea about the importance of breathing for my recovery. I often spent hours sitting in front of my computer, stressed and over-stimulated, slouched and stutter breathing, amplifying my anxiety and making it worse by the hour. It's easy to see how this was a major factor in my troubles.

Anxiety attacks are a great example of the vicious cycle that adrenaline can create. It starts when your mind is racing (from too much caffeine, perhaps!) and you start to stress. When you start to stress and worry, you lose focus on your breathing, and you start taking short, shallow breaths. As a result, your adrenaline begins to rise. Now your anxiety becomes worse, which makes your breathing even worse. Your breaths become even shorter, faster, and more stressful. Soon, you're in a full-blown attack.

However, if you can snap yourself out of that spiral and modify your breathing at any point in the cycle—slowing down to take long, deep breaths—you can start to bring yourself relief.

In the case of general anxiety (aka stress from a busy day), you can experience relief with just one to three minutes of slow, controlled breathing. I recommend six to eighteen deep breaths done while sitting upright in your chair—four seconds inhaling and six seconds exhaling, on each breath. It's amazing how quickly you can shift your physical and mental state through this type of breathing.

The irony, of course, is that when people are anxious, they often feel like they *can't* breathe. They find it difficult to slow down and take big deep breaths into the belly, and so they try harder, stepping up the *speed* of their shallow, upper-chest breathing, which only makes it worse. But deep, controlled breathing is the healthy, anxiety-reducing way to go. And if you struggle with our next topic, sleep, this type of slow breathing is also a great way to knock you out fast.

Sleep Your Way to Safety

Each night during my struggles with anxiety I'd turn on classical music to calm me down, and then hope and pray for sleep to take me soon. While it worked on Bally (like all dogs, he never had any trouble falling asleep), I tossed, turned, and stared at the ceiling for at least an hour.

Getting a good night's sleep, or any sleep at all, can be a serious challenge for people dealing with anxiety.

Interestingly, this is where the chain reaction of positive habits begins to yield exponential results, because deep breathing techniques can not only reduce your anxiety but also improve your ability to fall asleep. The Harvard-educated celebrity doctor Andrew Weil advocates this deep breathing technique, which can be used to reduce anxiety and fall asleep:

- Breathe in for four seconds

- Hold your breath for seven seconds

- Breathe out for eight seconds

If you repeat that twice, you'll calm down; and if you use that cycle for as little as four repetitions, you'll fall asleep faster. I know, it sounds so simple that it's almost unbelievable, but it's worked for me (in my post-anxiety days) many times.

Sunshine is another factor in how well you sleep. If you get yourself out into the sunshine early in the day, you're getting your body's clock in alignment. That's another reason that an early morning walk is so helpful in fighting off stress and anxiety.

And if I could go back in time and give my younger self just one piece of advice about sleep, it would be this: **Go to sleep and get up at the same time every day (seven days a week)**—ensuring that you get the sleep you need on a daily basis—you'll avoid building a sleep deficit, and you'll have more energy each day. It's boring, but it works.

You might believe that if you sleep in on the weekend, you'll catch up on the sleep you lost throughout the week. Unfortunately, it doesn't work that way. Your sleep deficit builds over time, and it takes much more than a couple of weekend mornings to eliminate this deficit and the constant feeling of being tired.

It should be no surprise that caffeine and other stimulants prevent most people from falling asleep. In my book, *The Perfect Day Formula*, I make the case for cutting out all caffeine ten hours before bed, but when you don't sleep well because anxiety keeps you up all night, you often find yourself relying on caffeine to keep you going through the day. And while your morning joe might bring some sense of relief, if you keep going back to the coffee well throughout the afternoon, you're going to pay the price when you toss and turn and lie in bed at night, giving your mind more fuel to keep it racing and revving the anxiety engine. One of the first things you should do if you struggle to get to sleep at night is start tracking your caffeine intake. Cut back on those big Starbucks drinks, switch to lower-caffeine alternatives, and restrict your intake to early in the day.

Alcohol is another controversial contributor to poor sleep. You might think that glass (or two or three or four) at night takes the edge off and helps you fall asleep, but the alcohol is proven to impair deep sleep cycles overnight. That's why a little booze might help you get to sleep on time so you get eight hours, but still leaves you waking up groggy (and anxious) the next morning. I recommend stopping all alcohol intake three hours before bed. While that sounds like I'm encouraging day drinking or daily visits to Margaritaville (hey, even when you have anxiety it's 5 o'clock somewhere!), I'm not. What it really means is that you should take a serious look at minimizing or completely eliminating your alcohol consumption as you build healthy new habits aimed at reducing stress and anxiety.

Like each individual strategy we've discussed so far, breathing and sleep alone won't rid you of anxiety forever. However, when you get enough sleep and you breathe properly, you'll increase your chances of avoiding anxiety. Breathing and sleep complement the other tools in your anti-anxiety toolkit, and they lay the foundation for the two powerful, life-changing habits we'll discuss in the next chapter: yoga and meditation.

Exercise: Make the Introspection Connection

This is an exercise I teach to my coaching clients at our 1-day workshops. At the end of your workday, right after dinner, or about an hour before bed, sit back and review your day. Compare what you wanted to do against what actually happened.

For example, let's say you wanted to wake-up on time, write 500 words for a project, meditate, get the kids to school, arrive at work on time, have a day full of meetings, take a walk at lunch, and get back home at 6 p.m. on time for dinner.

What really happened was that you woke-up and had a big, Starbucks-style coffee. That helped your writing, but ruined your meditation (because your mind was racing), and left you snapping at the kids. You were anxious in your meetings (where you had another coffee), and your team could sense it. You took on more projects than necessary at work (the caffeine made you do it!), skipped your lunchtime walk, had a post-lunch energy crash (justifying one more espresso), and you ended up working till 6:30 p.m., getting you home an hour late for dinner. By then you were stressed and needed a glass of wine to take the edge off. After family dinner and putting the kids to bed, you sat down with your (2ⁿᵈ) glass of wine, and watched the movie of your day. This is where you establish cause-and-effect between the caffeine and the havoc it caused in your day. From there, you realize you need to resolve to cut back on over-consumption of caffeine early in the day, otherwise the domino effect is going to bring you more stress and anxiety, poor performance at work, and less peace at home at night. Because that's easier said than done, you also realize you need to seek accountability to hold you to these new boundaries, and if you get that from a friend or a coach, you'll make a significant change that will lead to more success. That's the power of this simple little introspection exercise, and you can apply to every area of life.

Summary

- Breathing and sleep are underrated tools for helping you fight off stress and anxiety.

- If you're feeling stressed, sit back, slow your breathing, and you can change your physiology in just a minute or two. Keep this secret weapon at the ready for traffic jams, stressful meetings at work, or visits to the in-laws.

- Eliminate caffeine 10 hours before bed, and stop drinking alcohol 3 hours before bed. These two changes will help you fall asleep and stay asleep, so that you aren't stressed or anxious when you start your mornings.

CHAPTER 6

YOGA AND MEDITATION

"Buddha was asked: "What have you gained from Meditation?" He replied: "Nothing." "However", Buddha said, "let me tell you what I lost: Anger, Anxiety, Depression, Insecurity, Fear of Old, Age and Death."

– AUTHOR UNKNOWN

I did my first yoga class before wearing yoga pants to work, church, or job interviews was considered normal. It was January 4th of 2006, just days after my original anxiety attack. A friend at the gym where I was a personal trainer set aside an hour and generously took me through one of the most calming hours of my life. I've been chasing the dragon ever since, trying to recreate the peace I felt as I lay on the mat at the end of our session. While I haven't quite found it, that yoga session was a big step in the right direction for my healing from anxiety, and it remains a daily practice that keeps excess stress away.

Of course I did what most stubborn, busy Type-A people do when they find something relaxing that works. I stopped doing it. What stopped me was probably the same thing stopping you from taking up any of the Eastern arts to calm your Western anxiety. We have a misperception that yoga, and its cousin, meditation, need to be huge time commitments, and you might even think you need to join a cult, and start wearing the JP Sears-approved tribal outfit (stretchy pants, tank top with motivational phrase, headband, etc.). But it doesn't have to be like that—you can get substantial benefits from even just a few minutes of yoga or meditation each a day in the comfort of your own home, wearing whatever you'd like (baggy sweats and 10-year old, uncool t-shirts included – bonus points for hard rock concert t-shirts!). A little bit goes a long way for both these disciplines, and the benefits extend far beyond the physical.

With both yoga and meditation, most of the anxiety-reducing benefits come from the technique we discussed in the last chapter: better breathing. The yoga-meditation-breathing style leads to breakthroughs that keep you calm and keep your anxiety in check. If you feel you really can't sit there and just do breathing exercises on your own, you can also try some type of guided meditation (there are plenty of excellent ones available for free on YouTube – Pro Tip: always go with one where the voice is a British accent). If you don't like sitting still, give yoga a shot. Either way, if you're like many people, you'll quickly come to love the benefits that both meditation and yoga deliver once you try it, especially if you get a great instructor. I was hooked on the idea, if not the practice, of yoga high from my first time thanks to a patient, caring teacher.

I've also tried tai chi and qigong, as I mentioned earlier. These are less common Eastern disciplines that work just as well. In the end I decided they just weren't for me, but perhaps with better instructors and taught to me in a different environment, they might have stuck like my yoga and meditation habits of today.

The scientific benefits of meditation and yoga are indisputable. A 2005 German study on the benefits of yoga was summarized in the April 2009 blog post "Yoga for Anxiety and Depression" published on the Harvard Medical School's website. In only ninety days of yoga classes (twice a week), the study's participants reported improvements in "perceived stress, depression, anxiety, energy, fatigue, and well-being," according to the post. In the course of just three months of yoga, the study's participants improved their depression scores by *fifty percent* and their anxiety scores by *thirty percent*. In addition, the "initial complaints of headaches, back pain, and poor sleep quality also resolved much more often in the yoga group than in the control group," according to the study.

Meditation and yoga help you control your internal state. If you're able to control your internal state, you're able to move away from all the physiological conditions associated with anxiety, including increased blood pressure, heart rate, adrenaline, and stress levels.

Yoga, meditation, qigong, and tai chi are all are based on principles of mindfulness and breathing. That is what you're looking for—better awareness and better breathing—because those will both help you calm down.

Meditation is a practice that I have done daily for over five years. It's also something I can do on my own schedule. I don't have to travel and show up at a specific place at a specific time, which gives meditation a huge advantage of many other activities.

At first, I struggled with meditation, which is common for beginners. There were two things I did that helped me make it a habit. First, I started with just two minutes. Once I was comfortable with that, I bumped it up to three, eventually settling on a habit of 10-15 minutes per day. Second, everything changed for the better when I shifted my mindset to focus on the benefits instead of the difficulties. Instead of thinking, "Okay, I'm going to try to sit here for ten minutes," I started focusing on the benefit. "Notice how good you feel when you do this," I would remind myself. Once I made that shift, I was able to stick to meditation. The practice of meditation is so enjoyable that it can become a reward, as well as a habit.

The beauty of yoga and meditation is that you can get started quickly and easily and get the benefits from each today. Even if you're not sure about some of these tools, you should still give them a try—preferably with the best in-person instructor you can find at first, just to make sure you're doing things properly. That said, technology has made all of these practices much easier to start, with countless online videos and mobile applications. Headspace, one of the most popular apps in the world, provides free guided meditations and mindfulness training, for instance.

I was once that kind of guy that laughed at the idea of yoga and meditation. But my anxiety attacks, and the results I had from these Eastern practices, opened my eyes and changed my mind. Billions of people aren't wrong about these practices. They truly can—and will—change your life and reduce your stress and anxiety. This book is intended to guide you—gently—out of your comfort zone. The payoff is a life where you control your anxiety, instead of a life where anxiety controls *you*. If you're reading this, it means all the other things you tried in the past didn't work—that's why you're here. Yoga and meditation are two of the most beneficial ways to better your breathing and mindfulness to prevent or reduce your anxiety and live a life of calm and peace.

Taking a holistic approach to attacking your anxiety, including the use of yoga, meditation, better breathing, consistent exercise, and real-food nutrition will benefit you, even if you don't adopt all of them to the extremes. Again, none of these techniques will single handedly cure your anxiety, so it's important to put as many of these habits into place as possible.

Mindfulness 101

When was the last time you actually slowed down, put away your phone, took a deep breath and drank in your surroundings? We often do this on vacation, sitting at a table overlooking the Amalfi Coast, or maybe after an early-morning hike up in the Alps or Rockies to catch a view of the breathtaking landscape below. These moments of mindfulness don't have to be reserved for once-in-a-lifetime vacations. They can, and should, happen every day.

Mindfulness is an outcome of meditation, yoga, and similar practices, including daily self-reflection and introspection. It is about being conscious and present; about slowing down and not rushing. It's also about being aware—aware of yourself, of others, of how you feel, of how others feel.

It has always been a challenge for humans to be present and mindful, and more so in today's digital age than ever. Research shows that even if a mobile phone is simply placed on a table, it increases distraction and reduces focus when two people are having a conversation. Of course, these days it's rare to find a phone-free table, and it's not uncommon to see friends and even families ignoring one another while giving their attention to their phones. But almost every time we use our phone, it stimulates our mind, leads to stress, and ultimately, anxiety.

Most people don't know how to slow down and be present in a way that helps them process information more effectively. Meditation trains you to be present, slow your pace, and be mindful. This process of meditating and being mindful will allow you to control your breathing and control your state. When you finish your meditation and enter a state of mindfulness, you'll be less impatient, and you won't be rushing around. This, in turn, ties in naturally with anxiety reduction. It all sounds so easy, doesn't it? So then why isn't everybody using these solutions to change their lives, eliminate stress, and reduce anxiety? I discovered the answer to this question after working with clients for nearly twenty years in the fitness industry. When I would talk to someone who expressed a desire to get back in shape, but was doing nothing about it, I asked why.

The most common answer was this: they believed that exercise was effective, worked for other people, and would even work for them. Similarly, people believe that meditation, yoga, and mindfulness work for other people, and would work for them. So what's the problem?

They believe these methods work, but they *do not believe they will follow them*. To put it bluntly, they don't believe in themselves. This belief is usually based on past experiences, specifically—what people view as past attempts that ended in failure.

I experienced the same thoughts when taking up meditation. I first tried making it a daily habit after my first anxiety attack. While it helped me improve my breathing, I could never make it stick. Three years later I tried again, got frustrated, and gave up. I knew it worked, I knew it could work for me, but I just didn't believe in myself. Finally, on January 31st, 2013, while staying at the Viceroy Hotel in St. Petersburg, Florida, I made the decision to make meditation a habit, no excuses. I started with two minutes that day, using everything I had learned from mentors and past attempts. I haven't missed a day since, simply because I changed my mind and finally started believing that I could do it.

The big lesson here is that you must never accept these limiting self-beliefs in any area of your life. The experiences you view as failures were attempts, perhaps, that you gave up on too soon, or they may have been valuable learning experiences. The activity may have not been in alignment with your values and vision in your previous attempts. Most importantly, those past struggles have no bearing on who you are right now. Sometimes for change to happen, you must first change what you believe about yourself.

Be a Mindfulness Rebel

Yoga and meditation are both effective for me, and although I don't do yoga classes regularly, I do spend fifteen minutes per day on my own going through a few poses for my physical and mental health. Today, meditation is the tool I use most. It has helped me become more patient and more mindful. It's helped me slow down, breathe better, think more clearly, become more reflective and introspective, and make wiser decisions.

When I meditate, I break a few traditional rules. I sit in a chair in a dark room, usually just before sunrise, close my eyes, and breathe slowly for ten to fifteen minutes. I use no apps, and I'll never attain the Lotus position, but this works fine for me. There are many forms of meditation, so keep experimenting until you find the type that works best for you. You'll know which methods to pursue based on the sense of calm and peace you feel when you're finished. If you go into meditation believing that it can only done in one certain way, or that it must be done for a long period of time to "work," it becomes much more difficult to stick to it. I like to remind people that

I started with only two minutes of meditation in my very first session. Two minutes. The next week I extended my practice to three minutes. Each time, I was counting my breaths, aiming for at least one hundred. "Just a few more," I thought in my early sessions, and that got me through to the end and helped meditation become a consistent daily habit—one that I haven't missed since I started - even though sometimes I've had to meditate in airports, on airplanes, and even in my office just to get my "fix".

So go ahead and break the rules. Do mindfulness your way. All that matters is results. As you get better at being mindful, you'll start to notice what activities calm you down and make you feel at peace. Is it a walk in the park? Is it yoga at night? Is it yoga in the morning? Is it meditation at lunchtime? Try a variety of things to figure out which ones you enjoy the most, and which ones you want to stick with. There's no magic metric or rule when it comes to evaluating what activities make you happy. You'll just know it when you find it.

The great news is you have the flexibility to decide what is best for you, and how you will put it into practice. You don't have to spend four hours a day at this. Just begin with a few minutes per session at a minimum, do it consistently, and you'll soon begin to see and feel the positive and healthy benefits.

Yoga, meditation, or any other activity you choose will then join nutrition, diet, and other anxiety-reducing strategies in your toolbox. Healthy eating and nutrition were never really a problem for me, but there have been other big changes in my life, like cutting back dramatically on alcohol—I now only have one or two drinks a week. I go outside more. I sleep very well. I have also backed off from exercise a tiny bit, in the spirit of moderation. Years ago, I was one of those people who get anxious about missing workouts. Now I don't worry about it at all and have come to realize there are benefits to giving your mind and body a break from intense training.

On a ten-point scale, my anxiety level today is probably a two, now that I've made these positive changes in my life. The biggest revelation has been the knowledge that there was nothing wrong with me, and that I could build a powerful toolbox of easily accessible tools and habits to control my anxiety, fight off future attacks, or "cure it" entirely.

I've now given you these tools, strategies, and secrets that will do the same for reducing your stress and anxiety: breathing, meditation, yoga, tai chi, qigong, consistent exercise, healthy nutrition, and cutbacks in caffeine and alcohol.

The black box of anxiety will always be there for others, but it will no longer be as mysterious or scary to you. That's because you know exactly what's in it, how to open it, and what to do to fix it and defend yourself against it. You may still have to confront your anxiety from time to time, but when it surfaces, you can say, "No problem. I've got this." That is a powerful and reassuring position to be in.

Next, we'll explore how to leverage this newfound power to become an even more skilled, strong, and powerful warrior against your anxiety. To do this, you will now need to change something else: *your mindset.*

Exercise: Mini-Mindfulness

Stop. Put the book down. Pick your preference and have a mini-mindfulness moment. Take up yoga or meditation for the next two minutes. Breathe slowly and deeply. Feel the calm and relief rush over you. Two minutes was not so bad, was it? Imagine how you'd feel if you did this daily. Imagine what life would be like if you could, like I did, take your anxiety down from a ten to a two? Once you're done, finish the rest of this book and then make mindfulness a daily habit in whatever way suits you best. There are more options than excuses, and it's to make this work.

Summary

- Yoga and meditation are more popular than ever for a reason: They work. Set aside any stigma you have and make time for what matters – you.

- Ask your friends for a referral to a great beginner yoga class or go online and use one of the many guided meditations. Give each just a few minutes per day and build them into your daily habits for long-lasting relief.

- Finally, be mindful. Take a minute each day to be without stimuli or stress, and simply sit and be aware of how far you've come in life.

BEING UNSTOPPABLE EVERY DAY

―――

In Part Three, we dive deeper into deciphering the mysterious black box of anxiety and show you how to escape it through social support, positive influences, happier habits, and developing the right perspective about challenging situations in life.

Each of these approaches will immediately reduce your stress levels and shift your mindset in a positive and powerful way.

In Chapter Seven, *An Unstoppable Perspective*, you'll learn about a simple technique that changed my life, taking me from having a black heart to a light mind. When you turn this into a daily habit, anxiety will have a hard time holding on to a place in your heart. The next thing that needs to change is your environment. You can't soar with eagles if you hang around turkeys. If the people you meet and places you go are stressing you out, something needs to change to make your hero's journey easier. This might mean some tough decisions and difficult conversations, but in Chapter Eight, *Unstoppable Influences*, I'll show you how to get ahead – even without leaving everyone you love behind.

Finally, in Chapter Nine, *Your Unstoppable Journey*, you'll be given the final steps to follow on your path back to peace, and keep anxiety away for good. You'll then be able to live a life of true freedom again, knowing that whatever obstacles come your way, you'll always have the tools, support, and strength be anxiety free every day.

CHAPTER 7

AN UNSTOPPABLE PERSPECTIVE

*"Gratitude is the healthiest of all human emotions. The
more you express gratitude for what you have, the more
likely you will have even more to express gratitude for."*

– ZIG ZIGLAR

If anxiety was the stake to my heart, envy has always been my
Achilles heel. What I'm about to share is probably an even
more embarrassing story than the one of my anxiety attacks,
but telling you is an important part of my recovery, and so the
tale must be told. It takes place on a hot, sunny Sunday, July
22nd, 2012. Bally the Dog and I were out visiting my mother on
the farm where I grew up. Going through my email, I found
a message from one a good friend and business colleague,
Vince Del Monte.

"Craig," Vince wrote with his typical enthusiasm, "I just launched a new program. It's crushing it. Just wanted to let you know in case you wanted to promote it."

A normal person would have smiled, congratulated Vince, maybe threw in some "high-five" emojis, and sent a nice message back. Not me. Instead, my heart turned black with envy, and I – shamefully – said to myself, "That should be me. Vince is the one who came to my seminar, he's my student, and I should be making more money than him." What a horrible thing to think, I know. Fortunately, my deepening ability to engage in mindfulness and introspection made me aware of my flaw and I decided to do something about it.

Somewhere in my mother's house I found a thank you card and wrote out a note to Vince, thanking him for being a great husband and father, a role model and mentor in the fitness industry, and I listed everything that I loved about "Vinny D." This simple act flipped a switch in my mind, turning my black heart and envy into a smile on my face and lightness in my heart. What started off as something bitter turned into something better.

I hope envy doesn't have the same hold on you as it once did on me. But as with anxiety, these types of emotions can be overcome. Many of my clients, and almost every human alive, suffer from comparison syndrome, or what I labeled earlier as, "The number one first world problem."

Think about the last time you went on social media. Did you see someone who posted a picture about their "amazing holiday" or their new car, or them in a football stadium at the big game or a fun concert? How did it make you feel? Did you get all warm with gratitude for their good fortune? Or did it spark a little envy in your heart or jealousy in your belly?

It's okay, be honest. The former feelings still pop up in me from time to time. This syndrome is a natural human response, and for some reason we are wired that way. We always want more. The guy with the brand-new Ford F-150 XL wants the Ford F-150 Limited. The woman with ten pairs of shoes wants a dozen. The employee with the $5,000 raise wants $7,500. Nothing is ever good enough.

But it's not our fault. The real villain is the media's manipulation of our mind. The *New York Times* features articles on mindfulness and philanthropy right beside an advertisement for ten-thousand-dollar watches and handbags. Al Gore preaches environmentalism while owning ten-thousand-square-foot houses and flying across the country. He has a size seventeen carbon footprint. We're told to be happy with nothing, but oh by the way, you should buy all this stuff.

So you are tricked into taking on more projects, chasing more sales, commuting more miles, and sacrificing more of what really matters (time with your family, time for your health, etc.). And why? Because comparison means, that no matter how much we have, that we'll still never have enough.

The Antidote to Plunge Into Your Heart: Gratitude

To me, gratitude is the opposite of envy, a healthy response to feelings of comparison syndrome, and a habit that has had a massive impact on my life. Instead of wishing you had more stuff, gratitude makes you realize what matters, and helps you to be thankful for what you already have. When I started practicing gratitude, I realized that all the things I'm really happy for in life are so small and so inexpensive. You could take almost all of my money, and I'd still be able have the things that make me happiest – a dog, a gym membership, chocolate-covered almonds, books, and my family and friends. I remember vividly sitting there with my first gratitude journal, filling in the pages, and day after day writing, "I am grateful for this easy life." And life, or at least work, is easy now, compared to when I was thirteen years old and digging ditches all day in the hot sun for $3.10 an hour at my first summer job. If you had told me back then that I could sit behind a computer and sell workout programs for $60, let alone make millions of dollars per year, I'd have felt as though I won the lottery. Both envy and gratitude are simply a matter of perspective. One feeds your anxiety, and the other sets you free, and gratitude is a habit that you can use to soothe your soul.

You're already very familiar with the pleasure that gratitude can bring. Every year on Thanksgiving Day or at Christmas time, you get together with your family to celebrate. You're playing games, catching up with everyone, and having fun. You're eating good, simple, and delicious food. It's probably your favorite meal of the year, and far better than the most expensive dinner you had while in Vegas or New York or some other big city while on that work trip earlier in the year. And what's the cost of the food that seems to make us happiest on our holidays? A few dollars per person? As you can see, it's not the money that matters; it's something much deeper than that.

Thanksgiving Day is literally a day of thanks. Sure, you might be thinking about shopping or football and whatever else is on the agenda for the next day, but those plans are not what shape your true memories of the holiday. It's the time with family, the annual rituals, the giving of thanks, and the easy life that you're enjoying that day. You are celebrating the abundance you have, and aside from any anxiety around your annual awkward conversation with Uncle Kenny, you're probably all smiles and focused on the good in your life.

But here's the thing. Abundance and gratitude aren't these feelings that need to come but once a year. Gratitude can, and should, be a part of your life 365 days a year. It'll make you feel better, reduce your anxiety, and help you focus your mind externally on what matters, rather than internally where your wheels are spinning and causing stress. Making gratitude and thankfulness a daily habit changed my life, and it'll change yours too.

Write Your Way to Safety

I first heard about gratitude journaling from two of my earliest mentors, Yanik Silver, my second business coach, and Vishen Lakhiani, a very successful entrepreneur who runs Mindvalley. com. As I began to regularly journal about the many things I am thankful for, I began to realize how grateful I am for the easy life I have now. You see, I grew up doing manual labor on a farm from the age of eight. My first job away from the farm wasn't any easier, working outside year-round in the blistering heat or bitter cold at a local garden center. When I was sixteen years old, I spent an entire day outside painting, and that evening, surely suffering from heatstroke, I remember vomiting in the middle of a soccer game – a tough price to pay for the $40 that I had earned that day. Today, even though I've been up since 4 a.m. writing this chapter, my life is still exponentially easier, and for that I'm incredibly grateful. When you put things in the right perspective, like being grateful for a book deadline because you know the finished product has the potential to change millions of lives, suddenly what you're doing has far less power to bring you down.

Gratitude moves us away from envy, comparison syndrome, stress, and anxiety caused from spinning our mental wheels. While it's easy to get caught in the trap of thinking that your life is bad because your friend's business did $10 million last year while yours "only" broke the million-dollar mark, it should also be easy to remember that you've come a long way and that you're getting better every day.

But you can't overcome the toxic thoughts of envy or jealousy until you step back and start becoming grateful for how awesome your life is *now*. That's why gratitude journaling is so powerful—because it helps us do it every day.

When I first learned about gratitude journaling from Vishen and Yanik, I immediately began by writing down three things I was grateful for each day. It's so simple and something that you can do right now. Ask yourself this question, "What are three things I'm grateful for right now?" It could be your kids. It could be your dog. It could be sunshine. It could be chocolate-covered almonds. It could be how you felt after exercise, yoga, or sex! It could be the fact that you got out of bed early and wrote 500 words for your book. None of these are winning the lottery, but all of them will help you be thankful for the smallest (but most important) things in life and will put a smile on your face. My favorite part of my gratitude journaling is where I list all the people in my life who I appreciate. Some days my list goes on with dozens and dozens of names because I have so many friends that have made a difference in my life.

I've tried gratitude journaling first thing in the morning and last thing at night, and found that (for me, anyways) that using my gratitude journal at the end of the workday, after I have shut down my laptop, works best for me. Just five minutes of journaling each day will reduce your anxiety and help you sleep, because you'll end your day feeling so grateful for everything you have in your life. Pick a time of day and be consistent, turning this into a simple, yet powerful habit that helps keep your anxiety away.

Your gratitude journal also serves as a great reminder of what really matters. When you repeatedly write down that you're grateful for reading with your children, walking your dog at sunrise, being able to mentor someone at work, or taking time to have coffee with your mom and dad more often, these feelings of gratitude will soon spill over into directing how you spend your day, and you'll waste less time on social media worried about what other people are doing, killing that comparison syndrome

The gratitude journal is a reminder to focus on what matters, concentrate on what counts, and to align your actions with your goals so that you have less stress and more success.

The Unstoppable Gratitude Formula

Alright, you're thinking, writing in a gratitude journal sounds great, but how do I actually do it? In your gratitude journal, I recommend beginning with being thankful for what you accomplished that day (which is why I tend to do it at the end of the day). You could be grateful for closing a deal, writing a chapter in your book, finally having that difficult conversation at work, finishing a great work, or making time for a glass of wine with your partner. You can write down big things or little things, and you should be able to easily list three things you did over the course of the day that made you feel good. It might seem hard at first because you'll think these items have to be "Facebook-worthy." But they don't. Helping your child tie their shoe, or hearing the birds sing as you got into your car to go to work in the morning, putting on your comfy old sweatshirt on a chilly Fall day, drinking your morning cup of coffee from your favorite mug, or finding that last cold drink in the back of the fridge after a long run, all of these are worthy of putting pen to paper in your gratitude journal.

As you do this, you begin to realize you're grateful for many things that happen to you. You're grateful for people. You're grateful for your emotions. You're grateful for the memories you made. When you start to break it down like this, you suddenly think, "Wow, I can probably list fifty things and people that are positive in my life today." When you get to this point, this is when the magic happens. You experience a shift in your mindset from being internally focused and externally stressed to internally happy and outwardly engaged. This is a game-changer in being able to overcome anxiety for good.

Being thankful for your everyday life makes you realize how good you have it. While it's natural and good for us to strive for more, looking back, I was as happy making $40,000 a year as I am today. Back then I was grateful for my family, my friends, my health, and my dreams. Today, it's not much different. Sure there are a few more friends, and a few finer experiences, but I'm still grateful for so many small things in life, and I always try to remember that even back when I was broke, I was still living better than kings did three hundred years ago.

Gratitude journaling is part of the self-care solution, along with nutrition, meditation, and exercise. It acts as a balancing force in your life, one that helps you appreciate what you have to go with your ambition and motivation. It's like the yin and the yang. Ambition and motivation drive you forward, while appreciation and gratitude keep you grounded and are an effective way to attack anxiety.

If you would like to use the same gratitude journal I use on a daily basis, please visit Earlytorise.com/journal.

$1000 Thank You Therapy

Another way to show your gratitude and attack anxiety is to pre-emptively write and send thank you cards to your friends, family, and colleagues. I began doing this daily for years to fight off my embarrassing envy, change my mindset, appreciate my friend's triumphs, and to turn a toxic feeling into something positive.

My daily "Thank You Therapy" costs me over one thousand dollars per year in cards, postage, and time, but it's all worth it. I know each card puts a smile on someone's face – including mine. After all, it's rare to get a thank you card in the mail anymore (or anything good in the mail, for that matter).

As I put the thank you card in the mailbox, I look at the name on the envelope and say out loud, "Thank you." Not only do I feel good knowing the card will come as a pleasant surprise, I also know that each card sent crushed my envy into something insignificant. It also makes me realize, when comparison syndrome strikes, that that my life would be no better off if that person was not rich or not successful. In fact, the better their life is, the better *my* life is, because I believe that a rising tide lifts all boats, and that the more I surround myself with successful people (in all areas of life) the better I will become in business, in my relationships, and even in my fight against anxiety.

It's embarrassing to admit my past envy, and how acted as a paralyzing prison in my mind. But I'm grateful for my awareness about it, and my decision to fix it – just as you should be about any of your flaws that can be turned from adversity into advantage. It is this type of self-reflection and introspection that must be applied to your life so that you can take actions and attitudes that hold you back and turn them around into habits that help.

"If you don't like something," the author Maya Angelou said, "Change it. If you can't change it, change your attitude." Action beats anxiety. Action can also beat envy and any bad attitude. You can stay in an envious or negative mindset or you can change it and ask, "What could I do to overcome this feeling?"

Thank you cards might be the therapy missing from your life. You can start by writing one right now, do one per week, and then ramp it up to a daily habit. Or you can send a text or make a phone call. It doesn't matter how you deliver it, you just need to do it.

Adopting this new perspective on life didn't cost me any money, and it didn't hurt me in any way. It only made me better – and it will for you too.

Exercise: Write It Out Of Your Head From Your Heart

Start adding an "Attitude of Gratitude" or "Thank You Therapy" to your life right now. All you need is a scrap piece of paper and a pen to lighten your heart and mind. First, write down the first three things that come to your mind that put a smile on your face. Second, pick a friend, preferably one that you haven't spoken with in a long time, and write them a short Thank You note and put it in the post.

Summary

- Life doesn't have to be full of envy, comparison, stress or anxiety. One man's pleasure doesn't have to be another man's pain. Life is what you make it – and that comes from having the proper perspective.

- Spend time in introspection and self-reflection to see what mental habits cause you stress and anxiety. Find a way to flip the switch in your mind and turn adversity into advantage.

- Whether it's through writing thank you cards or keeping a gratitude journal, practicing gratitude will transform your life. You'll learn to be thankful for all of the good things you have and focus on the many great people around you. And when you're focused on those things, there's one thing you won't be focusing on anymore: anxiety.

CHAPTER 8

UNSTOPPABLE INFLUENCES

"When you take action, particularly bold action, the boundaries of what you believe to be possible (your belief system) expand. Which, in turn, gives you the capacity to consider new ideas, new possibilities, and new concepts that you previously thought to be impossible."

— ROBERT RINGER

"Fun Bobby" was a good friend of mine growing up throughout high school and college. He was at every party, often hosting them, rarely working, and always ready to drink, as long as the day ended in "y." Between school, work, and hitting the gym, I couldn't keep up with Fun Bobby at the bar, but I tried. And that was part of the problem that led to my anxiety. I was with Fun Bobby on the night of the final bender before my six-week heart attack began, and when it did, I knew something had to change. It wasn't easy saying goodbye to Fun Bobby, but it had to be done. Today Fun Bobby is still Fun Bobby, and spending time in the same bars telling the same stories and drinking the same drinks...well, it doesn't take a rocket scientist to see that would be a bad idea.

This was just one of the environments I had to leave in order to get healthy. You'll also need to make changes if you want to be anxiety-free, and that means creating coping strategies or eliminating the negative influences in your life. This might mean severing ties with toxic relationships, or it might mean building systems to tolerate people (i.e. relatives) that you simply can't completely cut out of your life. Making these changes might sound hard, but these tough decisions are absolutely critical to your health, sanity, and to success in business.

Think of your negative influences the same way an alcoholic needs to think about booze. If an alcoholic wants to stay sober, what do they do? First, they need to stop going to bars. Second, they must stop hanging around other alcoholics. Third, they should pour all the booze down the drain and never bring any more into the house. They should sell the margarita machine on E-bay and turn the channel when a beer commercial comes on. They have to develop strategies to avoid any mental or physical state that makes them crave a drink. Alcoholics must find new habits and hobbies to do at 5 o'clock so they don't get tempted to go to happy hour at "the local."

You need to do the same thing with anxiety. You need to deal with *everything* (and everyone) from your life that serves as a trigger for anxiety. You want to reduce the negativity and eliminate the external environments that stress you out.

Of course, I know what you're thinking. "That's impossible, Craig, I can't shut out my 'insert family member' here." And you're getting stressed out just thinking about eliminating all of your stress. I get it. I've been there. But I've also developed systems that allow me to enjoy the best of both worlds – family and freedom.

The solution begins with introspection. You need to sit back and reflect on what people and environments cause the most stress and anxiety in your life—and also identify what gives you relief. Once you do, the path forward is simple. Avoid the things that make you anxious and do more of the things that calm you down. Every day you must move to eliminate the triggers and add more routines and habits that support your success and reduce stress.

To accomplish this, you *must* put certain boundaries in place. If heavy traffic gives you extreme anxiety, you *must* leave work earlier, so you don't get caught in traffic. If your friends drag you into bad situations on Saturday nights but are otherwise good friends, then make a rule to see them during the week or on Saturday morning, but not on Saturday night. If listening to your well-meaning, but ranting Uncle Kenny makes you angry, you need to figure out ways to control the conversation, or see your way out of any interactions that leave you uncomfortable. And if your current business gives you massive anxiety, then you have to make hard decisions about what you are willing—and not willing—to do in order to be successful. Simply put, you need to align your actions and your goals, and you must look at every environment you're in as your personal responsibility. But make no mistake, if you do what you've always done, you'll get what you've always had.

Listen, there were a lot of tough decisions I had to make at age 30 when my anxiety sent me to the emergency room. Well, at least they seemed tough then, but in hindsight, they were decisions I should have made five years earlier. And with a little time and space you'll likely come to the same conclusion about the choices that lie in front of you.

I had to cut ties with drinking buddies and girls that were no good for me. I also had to start saying "no" more often and put boundaries into my work life (although, ironically, what I found, as most of my clients also do, is that once you step back and start working with a better plan you actually achieve more in less time than you did before). I also had to start living in alignment with my values and vision, and the right rules for my right life, a set of standards that were always in my mind, but that I had chosen to resist when I was out of alignment.

When I finally took my own advice that you see here in this book, everything changed. The weight of the world was lifted from my shoulders. I could breathe again, I could think again, and I could move fast and free again thanks to finally focusing on what really mattered to me: helping others transform their lives, rather than wasting my nights in bars and days in bed.

The difficult choices you must make in life ultimately result in true freedom. Structure in your day will break the bonds of being a slave to your work. Hard decisions will unshackle the handcuffs that keep you anxious and unsure every day. Removing the negative influences in your life will set you free.

All that said, you can't—and shouldn't—remove everything that stresses you in life. There are many positive challenges that actually make you better and stronger. You need to identify these and make sure you keep them in your plan, so you can lean into life and grow. For example, this might include networking at seminars, doing public speaking, becoming a better listener at work, or learning new skills like filming videos to promote your business. You might even need to buy that dog and deal with those nights where your puppy causes you more anxiety, because you know in the long run that you've found a new best friend that will change your life (I know I did, and it was worth all the effort). These are all areas where I've put my energy since taking back control of my life. You shouldn't avoid personal or professional growth just because it's stressful, because that would be a step backward from your goal of connecting with like-minded, positive people. You have to lean into positive stress, because that supports the right decisions for your best life.

If you're still not sure what to change in your life, think about it this way: Imagine your life was a friend's life. Now look, with outside eyes, at what "your friend" is doing, and who they are doing things with, and think about the advice you would give them. The solutions become a lot clearer when you remove the emotion and attachment from difficult decisions, don't they? Any mature adult could see that my weekend behaviors were downright stupid, but I didn't want to admit it. Unfortunately for me it took a massive anxiety attack to open my eyes, and I don't want that to happen from you. When you know something is the right decision, do *not* run from it. Lean in and do the work.

Cutting Toxicity and Time Vampires

There's a story in my book *The Perfect Day Formula* about how, if you place a bunch of crabs in a bucket, one of the crabs will try to climb out of the bucket and escape, but the others remaining in the bucket will *always* pull the ambitious one back down.

In Australia, they have something similar they call "tall poppy syndrome," where the most successful people (the tallest poppies) are resented and get cut down by others. Germany has something called schadenfreude, which is when someone gets pleasure from the suffering of another. It's human nature, due to something gone wrong in our wiring, that leads us to gossip, talk behind other people's backs, and to try and lift ourselves up through the process of bringing others down. Obviously, this is a behavior you need to cut from your habits, but it's also something you'll need to cope with when others do it to you.

Sit down and make a list of all the people who hold you back in life, including those who are well meaning but don't support you and those who actively sabotage your efforts by cutting you down, and begin to build coping strategies so that you do everything possible to avoid them. Just like the alcoholic (i.e.

me) who needs to delete the text messages from his old drinking buddies (i.e. Fun Bobby), you need to do all that you can to stay out of toxic relationships and negative environments. It's going to be hard at first, but eventually these people will find someone else to talk about, and you'll become an afterthought in their lives while being more successful in yours.

One type of stress-inducing character in nearly all of our lives is known as the "time vampire." This person needs to go on your "avoid at all costs" list. Time vampires are, obviously, those people who suck up an excessive amount of your day in wasted conversations, unnecessary meetings, or plain old gossip. While they might be happy to waste their lives, do *not* let them steal yours. You can guard against this by creating coping strategies, such as better planning for your day so that you already have your time blocked for more productive behaviors, and also setting appropriate expectations in every communication.

For example, when a toxic time vampire comes to suck away the next hour of your life, tell them, "Hey, I've only got five minutes. Let me know how I can help, but I'll have to go soon because I have an important call." Or let them know that you have a ten-minute block open two days from now, saying, "Let's put this on our calendars now and limit it to ten minutes, because I know you're busy and I don't want to waste your time." Setting clear expectations for every communication, from phone calls to meetings, respects everyone's time and is one simple way to keep stress and anxiety at bay.

The harsh reality is that we often willingly let time vampires into our lives when we're tired and want to take the easy way out. It's 3 o'clock, you've been up and working non-stop since six in the morning, and wouldn't it be nice just to "shoot the breeze" for a few minutes? Going down that path of least resistance often leads to the slippery slope of bad decisions, and the next thing you know you're an hour behind on your work. It's no different than mindlessly scrolling through the notifications on your phone, looking for something to distract you from the work you do not want to do. But if you think about the most positive, high-achieving people in your life, you'll notice they don't have a lot of time to spare. They don't let time vampires steal from their busy schedule, and you can't either.

Stay Out of the Social Media Rabbit Hole

I still remember the day in 2006 when I finally decided to change my morning ways. I woke up "late" at 7:30 a.m., already feeling anxious like I was chasing the tail of the world. I rolled over in bed, reached for my Blackberry (remember those?), and started checking my email. Out of twenty messages, nineteen were positive, but one was a critical comment that put it me in a bad mood for the rest of the day. My mind raced, my wheels turned, and I wasted hours thinking of all the snarky replies to send back. Essentially, I had lost the day before it had even begun, and my stress and anxiety levels showed. "Never again," I said. Later that day, I removed email from my phone and started building systems and habits that enabled me to avoid the Internet for hours every morning, so I could do the deep work that moves me ahead (such as writing this book) while leaving stress and anxiety behind. As soon as I get up my phone goes into airplane mode and gets put into a drawer while I work, and I've turned off notifications for all apps, removing all distractions and temptations so I can stay on track.

Take a look at your morning. If you wake up and get sucked into the "rabbit hole of the red dot," losing the first thirty to sixty minutes of your day to anxiety-inducing social media, fake news, or gossipy text message conversations, then you've found a significant source of much of your stress.

Here's the cold harsh truth about the so-called "smartphone" in your hand: It's been designed to be an addiction. It's not your fault. That's right, tens of thousands of the cleverest minds in the world are working every day in Silicon Valley to keep you glued to your phone. Those red notification dots, one of the most infamous inventions of the 21st century, have turned us into the equivalent of a cocaine-addicted lab rat seeking its next hit from pushing on a lever. Your phone has taken over your life and you're on the verge of a breakdown because of it, and it's time for this to end. Listen, I'm not against all social media or technology; in fact, I think it can be very helpful for both your business and your personal life. However, it must be used properly, and that generally starts with resetting your relationship with your phone.

You need to avoid your *online* triggers of anxiety, especially early in the morning. First, again, enter introspection mode. Whose posts get you fired up? Now you must make the decision to remove or block them. Next, cut your intake of news to next-to-nothing, unfollow (or unfriend) Facebook friends that give you even an ounce of anxiety, delete as many apps as you can from your phone, and turn off those red dot notifications (listen, you're not going to "forget" to check social media, so it's not like you need a reminder showing up on your phone all day long).

If you feel you must continue to check the news, make a rule that you don't check it until you have accomplished a block of deep work on your most important task in the morning. But the harsh truth is that you simply don't need to check the news. If something major happens, you'll hear about it from a friend, or people talking about it in public. If something terrible has happened halfway across the world, it won't change anything in your life today (or tomorrow, or likely ever), and obsessing about it can keep you from achieving your goals. Additionally, the news media has been engineered to increasingly make us fearful, so we'll become even more addicted to their shocking headlines and ridiculous, yet irrelevant stories and return to their sites and channels for more information.

You won't miss it once you leave this daily drama behind, and in a few weeks, or even days, you'll look back and shake your head at how much time you were wasting being so engrossed in the life and opinions of other people. One of the reasons I love traveling to Europe every summer is because you get a reprieve break from CNN running the same story over and over again and claiming that the sky is falling. Of course, not everyone can travel halfway across the world when you get stressed, but you can take a weekend and go camping, or even a morning to go hiking, or simply to walk in a park for an hour without your phone. Unplug from the world, disconnect from the distractions, and you'll be reminded of and relieved about how your mind can—and should—operate.

Unplug From The Matrix and Set Your Mind Free

Unplugging from your devices makes the time vampires out in Silicon Valley nervous. They want you glued to the phone, and that's why they are using every trick in the book to do it. Research has shown that every time there is an alert or notification on your phone, you get a hit of dopamine in your brain. The more screens and apps you have, the more notifications you get, and the more addicted you become. Your mind races, playing Ping-Pong with each incoming alert, and it becomes a Pavlovian response, one that can last all day and night, if you let it. When your mind is always racing, constantly chasing all of those bings and buzzes, you're going to become very anxious, ineffective, and unproductive.

When we interact with friends on social media, it makes us feel good in the moment, but this reduces our desire for in-person, face-to-face interactions, which I'm convinced are far better and healthier for us in many ways. As a result, heavy social media use can actually make your anxiety *worse* because it gives the illusion of connection, but in truth, you're isolating yourself. You need touch. You need talk. There's no replacement for the feeling of having a hand on your shoulder or holding hands with somebody you love, or petting your dog (there will never be an app for that!). It's these in-person human (and doggy) connections that go a long way in helping you reduce your anxiety, and those types of communication can't happen online, no matter how many likes, loves, and shares—or even direct messages—you get. You are hardwired to seek out human contact, and it's very, very important for you to get that human touch, physically, mentally, and emotionally, especially when you have anxiety.

But Don't Block Me On Facebook Just Yet...

With all that said, this next section might surprise you. I'm a big believer in the power of *positive* social media. Social media doesn't have to be negative. In fact, I've made a point to set up all of my accounts so that all the social media I use is positive. Everything. I don't get any anxiety from social media, and here's how that happened: *I unfollowed everybody who caused me stress.*

If I see back-and-forth arguing and political debates, I eliminate those people from my feed. You can un-follow, un-friend, mute, or block every negative influence. I also don't get in arguments with anyone online, whether it's a friend with a drastically different political opinion or an unhappy customer. If it's the former, I shrug my shoulders and forget about it, and if it's the latter I do whatever it takes to create a happy customer. On Facebook, Twitter, LinkedIn, and Instagram, I only interact with people who post positive things. There are so many great sites to follow and people to follow, so if you're intentional and proactive in managing your feeds, you can turn social media into a very positive place. When you do that, then you'll start to see less of the crap, and less of the things that give you anxiety.

Here's another harsh truth: The data gods of Silicon Valley own your profile and know virtually everything about you. There's no more privacy, and aside from pulling a Thoreau and living in the woods, this is the reality you have to deal with. They know what pushes your buttons, and they put those things in front of you. They know what ads to run and what posts to serve in your timeline because those were similar to things that engaged you in the past.

However, you can use the power of their algorithms to bring you positive, healthy messages. You can accomplish that by unfollowing, unfriending, and not "liking" the posts and the people who incite feelings of anger, negativity, stress, or anxiety.

An example of the positive power of social media can be found from a University of Vermont study that showed checking into an online weight loss forum improved participants' results. There is power in positive social support—both offline and online—and you can harness that power by joining a membership site or Facebook group full of like-minded, supportive people. The more you check in, the more social support you get, and the more you'll continue your healthy behaviors and decisions.

If you get rewarded for doing something, you are going to do it more often. For example, our business has a "Perfect Day Formula" Facebook group. When our members check-in and say they woke up early and focused on their most important task first thing in the morning, other members congratulate them. When this happens, all members are much more likely to continue owning the morning and dominating their days.

It's powerful. Instead of being pulled down by others, you can find yourself surrounded by positive people who collectively help each other reach the top and escape the shackles holding them back in life.

My friend Joe Polish once said, "You can use social media, but don't let social media be used on you." I agree. If you don't groom your social feeds, you're going to get sucked into a negativity spiral. But if you have social feeds full of positive people, you'll be rewarded and inspired by your healthy insights and behaviors.

I can't stress it enough: you must proactively find and consume healthy, inspiring, positive information on a daily basis. Alwyn Cosgrove, a friend of mine from the fitness world, has a quote I love: "First thing to do every morning is read or listen to something positive. Your mind is like a garden—whatever you plant grows. Plant good stuff."

At the end of the day, even though the influences on your anxiety are most often external, *you* control your exposure to them. Your anxiety is *your* personal responsibility, just as your social media feed is your personal responsibility. If you want less drama in your life, stay away from situations with drama. If you want less anxiety, avoid the people and places (including those online) that trigger your anxiety.

Social media can be beneficial and healthy for everyone involved. You can build an entire career and make the world better by learning and contributing positive things to others.

Looking Back and Moving Forward

By this point in the book, you know that in order to achieve an anxiety-free life, you're going to need to reflect upon your life and assess the relationships you currently have. It's going to require difficult choices and hard conversations to figure out if you should even be hanging around certain individuals.

It's possible that you're going to feel guilt in the near future, when you realize, "I've known this friend for ten years, but I know I shouldn't hang around them now." If they're encouraging behaviors that lead to your anxiety, support your addictions, and risk putting you in the hospital, then you need take a break from that friendship until you have rules and coping strategies in place.

This is why you must do an audit of your life, focusing on what has caused (or prevented or eliminated) anxiety in the past. When doing your anxiety audit, list all the people in your life. Beside each of their names, put a positive mark or a negative mark. Negative marks are for people who cause you anxiety. You should spend less time with them or remove them from your life completely. A positive rating means that person reduces your anxiety. You spend more time with these people—talking, shaking hands, hugging, or anything at all.

In your anxiety audit, you should also list out foods, beverages, activities, and even pets. List them all and rate them all, so your anxiety audit reflects every factor possible, rates and ranks your triggers, and enables you to move further away from the causes of anxiety and closer to the solutions that will set you free. As I tell my clients, using another great quote from my friend Alwyn, "Every single thing you do moves you in one direction or the other: either closer to your goals, or further away from them."

It boils down to personal responsibility. While there may be a genetic component to anxiety, you can reduce your risk when you make the right decisions for your right life.

The teachings of Epictetus, a Stoic philosopher who lived over two thousand years ago, have been a big influence on my life and in my recovery from anxiety. The Stoics understood the power of auditing yourself; the idea of a daily reflection comes from Epictetus, who encouraged us to look at ourselves from an external point of view, in the third person. In other words, you need to watch the movie of your life.

Here's how that works. Let's say you felt really anxious today. One of the best things you can do is to take a few minutes right now to watch the movie of your life for the day, asking, "Why was I so anxious?" You might find that you had an interaction with a certain person that always makes you anxious, or that your rushed morning routine (from staying up late last night) put your day off to a bad start from which you never recovered, or that a late afternoon trip to Starbucks, where you treated yourself to a venti Frappuccino loaded with caffeine and sugar set you down the wrong road for the rest of your day. When you make watching the movie of your life a daily habit and reflect on what you see, the sources of stress and anxiety become very clear, and so should the next steps of eliminating the offending behaviors.

The problem in today's society is that few people engage in self-reflection and introspection. Few people are willing to take personal responsibility for their lives, and instead choose to blame other people, governments, political parties, and other organizations. If you switch your mindset and decide that everything in your life is *your* personal responsibility, then you'll gain true freedom toward making positive change. This freedom to change is one of the most powerful steps in overcoming anxiety. This is what drove me to try qi gong, yoga, meditation, and every option—while refusing to use prescription medications (because these would not fix the true cause of my troubles).

Once I learned and accepted that there was nothing physically wrong with me, I knew I could change my mental state. I realized that I had put myself into that mess, and I could get myself out of it. If people carried that mindset about everything holding them back—things like debt, anxiety, body weight, and more—this would be a different world, I'm convinced we'd all be more successful and more fulfilled. "Life's easy when you live it the hard way," my friend Dave Kekich said, "...and hard if you try to live it the easy way."

Action Beats Anxiety. Motion Beats Meditation. Work Beats Worry.

Remember: If you've been to the doctor and there is nothing wrong with you, that means you have the power to take control and responsibility over every aspect of your life.

While the suggestions in this book might seem tough, please remember that they come from a place of love. They come from a place of experience, from a man who was once in your shoes. I'm not preaching *down* to you—I'm walking *beside* you on your hero's journey, showing you that somebody cares, understands, and believes in your ability to break free of anxiety.

Avoid Self-Induced Solitary Confinement

With anxiety, the tendency is to feel like you need to isolate yourself until your anxiety passes. Please don't make that mistake. I did, and it only made things worse.

When I started having anxiety, I didn't tell anyone. I hid it, hid myself from others, and my anxiety only got stronger. My recovery process didn't start until I reversed course, opened up, and began telling others about my troubles, asking for help, and seeking others who had overcome it before. If you stay isolated, your situation will likely worsen (or at least won't get better) and you don't want that to happen.

If you're introverted by nature, it's easy to use that as an excuse to isolate yourself and retract into your shell. However, this is a trigger of anxiety, not a solution. It was only by cutting back on isolation and opening up to others that I was able to significantly reduce my anxiety.

Make Time For What Matters

Every single person I've ever coached has expressed a desire to spend more time with friends and family. Not a single one has ever said, "I wish I spent more time at home alone hunched over my phone!"

If the former—more quality time with others—is your goal, but your reality is more like the latter, then you need to draw the line and make some ruthless decisions about how you spend your time.

Setting boundaries on your time really hits home with parents who struggle to find time for their families. If you're one of these people, the reality of your boundaries will set in if you're willing to take an honest audit of your daily life. Look at how you spend the day. You might find that you're on email all the time, it's not limited in any way. Maybe you spend an hour taking calls from time vampires. You're likely not really putting in nine-and-a-half hours of work, and therefore, if you would cut back on some of those wasteful things, you could leave on time and get home to your kids.

Every minute you spend on ESPN.com or sending unnecessary email messages or arguing on Facebook is a minute you are stealing from your kids. You get home and your children are crying because you're late again, and you feel guilty. You can eliminate a lot of that by making the right decisions over the course of the day. In most cases, that means putting down the phone, unsubscribing from emails, and unfollowing people on Facebook.

With those lines you're currently drawing—six hours of sleep and twenty email subscriptions—why not move that line back even a little bit further? Go to bed an hour earlier to make it seven hours of sleep so you're better rested. Subscribe to only three email newsletters. Put the phone down more, and say, "I'm not going to check my phone more than once an hour."

You can't just put your phone on standby and set it on the table at dinner—you need to turn off your notifications or put the phone away. You have to completely forget about your phone and be fully present. It's possible to do. Before the era of smartphones, we were all able to get through the day without having a phone in front of us constantly.

You have to draw the line, set boundaries, go to the extreme to use your time on the right things so you have less anxiety. If you'll redraw those lines and set boundaries around your time, you'll suddenly find you've reclaimed several hours per day, to use more happily or productively in your life. Now you'll be able to get home on time, and you won't be stealing quality time from the people who matter to you.

When you make these tough decisions and set the right boundaries, your journey gradually becomes easier and more enjoyable.

Exercise: Cut Back to Get Ahead

What you don't do is often just as, if not more important than what you do. Giving up bad habits, removing yourself from the wrong environments, and spending less time with certain people will give you a lot of relief in life. Pull out a piece of paper and draw a line down the middle. Make a list of 'bad influences' on the left and 'good influences' on the right. Circle the top three on each side, and commit, for the next seven days, to spend more time with the people and in the places that help you, and less time with the things that don't. Do this every week for three months, and you'll make a dramatic difference in your life.

Summary

- Things change and people change, and you can't be afraid to move ahead and leave stuff behind if it's required for you to get healthy again and live your best life. Don't feel bad for outgrowing people that had a chance to grow with you.

- Use social media, but don't let social media be used on you. Listen, Facebook and Instagram are designed to be addictive, but you can re-design them so your social media serves you. Don't let negative news or fake friends put anxiety into your life. Set up your systems so that you only plant good thoughts in your head each day.

- Take action. "If it is to be, it's up to me." Remember that motto. If you want your life to change, no one is going to do it for you. Take personal responsibility for where you are in life and how you feel. When you finally take ownership, it'll give you a freedom like you've never felt before.

CHAPTER 9

THE UNSTOPPABLE JOURNEY

"You have brains in your head. You have feet in your shoes. You can steer yourself any direction you choose. You're on your own. And you know what you know. And YOU are the one who'll decide where to go."

— DR. SEUSS

During the final two weeks of editing this book (a nearly full-time job in and of itself), I also had to hire four new team members, deliver five days of coaching in a row, record eleven podcasts, and fly across the country—twice. Oh, and my constant companion for the last twelve years, Bally the Dog, passed away.

But such is life. You and I will always feel like we're riding a rollercoaster, especially as an entrepreneur, with daily (and even hourly) ups and downs. Fortunately, as you continue to use and refine the processes detailed in this book, things will get better, and those tough times will never last.

Had I been faced with these external stresses in 2006, it's possible I would have reached for a drink and plunged into anxiety. But I have no fear of that today. I can handle more challenges than ever because I am armed with the knowledge that there's nothing wrong with me, and if I do feel a little stressed, I have two dozen coping strategies that I can pull out of my anti-anxiety toolbox to calm down, get back on track, and overcome any feelings of being overwhelmed. What bothered me over a decade ago no longer has control over me today, and soon you will feel that way too. The key is to understand that you have the power to prevent – and even attack – your anxiety because you are Unstoppable.

As you travel on your hero's journey in this epic battle for your life, you'll come across difficult choices that will need to be made both personally and professionally, but they will be worth it. Making hard decisions today sets you up for a lifetime of freedom where you'll finally able to put all of your energy back into things that matter..

We've talked about the hard reflection you have to do about your relationships, and the difficult decisions you'll need to make regarding who you spend time with. As you reduce the energy you give to negative relationships and increase the time you spend strengthening positive ones, your life will improve in many ways. As hard as it might be to imagine right now, there will come a time in the near future when you sit down, look back, and shake your head at how long you let some stressful things go on in your life. That's okay. We all have the temptation to remain in our comfort zones, to resist change, and to shy away from personal growth. However, as one of my favorite quotes goes, "If you want something you've never had, you must do something you've never done." Today's a good day to make that your motto in life too.

And while some of these decisions might seem hard, you need to trust the process that making the right decisions for your right life and going to turn out for the better. For example, many of my clients believe it's going to be hard to find good people in life who want to support them or join their team to grow their business. If you often find yourself thinking, "There are no good people out there who want to help me," it's time to take action toward reversing that belief. The truth is, there are a *ton* of great people who want to help you, and you can now redesign your life, so these positive people are the *only* ones you spend time with. If a socially awkward, introverted, former binge-drinker like me can do it, then you can too.

Choose Your Own "Hero's Journey"

As you move toward a life free of anxiety, remember that this is a hero's journey. There's no final destination with a finish line, balloons, rainbows, or unicorns—it's a lifelong journey, and one that will get more enjoyable every day.

Anxiety will always want to creep back into your life, but it won't as long as you have this roadmap to recovery with you. Make it an annual ritual to read this book from start to finish, to go through the alignment exercises, and to audit your healthy habits to make sure that you're still making the right decisions for your right life. Spend time in introspection and self-reflection identifying what you can do better and what habits need to be cut so that you stay successful and less stressful.

If you find yourself struggling in the future, one of the fastest ways to get back on track is to return to this book and review the proven anxiety-reducing behaviors and habits. In particular, focus on your breathing, give a little more time to meditation and yoga, and you'll quickly find yourself calming down. After that, check to see where bad habits are creeping back in and make any necessary adjustments.

No matter what happens in your life, remind yourself to *avoid isolation at all costs*. Get outside, spend more time your friends, and do whatever it takes to talk out your problems. The best remedy is to spend time with positive people and share what you're going through. Nothing is going to beat being with someone who cares about you, especially when they give you a simple hug or rub of your shoulders. Touch and talk are the most powerful antidotes to anxiety.

There can be no hero's journey unless there is adversity. And you cannot overcome adversity unless you take action. That's what the hero's do in your favorite movies, and now it's your turn to do that too.

How to Keep Anxiety Away—For Good

In your journey to keep anxiety from returning to your life, you'll need snappy, simple solutions to the five factors that cause most stress and anxiety in our lives: confusion, overwhelm, reactiveness, adrenaline, and isolation.

FACTOR ONE: CONFUSION

Confusion is the feeling you have when you don't know what's going on in your life, and you don't know how to deal with it. When you fail to plan, you plan to fail, and this creates anxiety. When you wake up without a plan in place for the day, then you'll be confused whether to start with the forty emails waiting for you, or the five voicemails, or scrolling through Instagram. None of these is the right choice, of course, and this confusion from a lack of planning adds fuel to the fire of your anxiety.

The simple solution to confusion is to reflect, plan, and prepare for tomorrow before you go to bed tonight. Proper planning prevents poor performance, and enables easy and automatic good decisions.

That's what reflection, planning, and preparation are all about—they help you avoid any confusion and quickly make the best decision for you.

FACTOR TWO: OVERWHELM

We all know the feeling of being overwhelmed, and it comes around when you've made too many commitments, have too many decisions to make, and have too much on your plate.

When there's too much going on—especially if you also add caffeine or other stimulants to the mix, and you're running late from hitting the snooze button—your brain can't handle the million different decisions it's being asked to make. This causes you to slip into panic mode, and the next thing you know you're breaking into a full-blown anxiety attack.

The simple solution is to eliminate temptations and distractions. Set your phone across the room so you have to get out of bed and so you'll be less tempted to hit snooze. Don't check your phone first thing in the morning or immerse yourself in the negative news. Say no to anything that does not serve you in a positive way.

Getting sucked in to drama and distractions serve as an escape, but they don't serve your purpose. And if you're looking for an escape, that means you are running away from your life—which is something you need to address and fix with the tools outlined in section one of this book. When you have a vision and are actively pursuing it, it will become easier to eliminate distractions and say no to everything that doesn't serve you.

FACTOR THREE: REACTIVENESS

Addressing the first two factors (confusion and overwhelm) will help you in attacking the third factor: being reactive. If you actually have a plan when you go into the office—to begin your morning working on one specific project, for instance—you don't have to be reactively doing anything else. You're being proactive, focusing on your most important project first. This helps you stay focused on the task at hand, move ahead, make progress, build momentum, gain motivation, and leave stress and worry behind.

FACTOR FOUR: ADRENALINE

If you're feeling stressed chances are you have higher than normal levels of adrenaline running through your veins. That often comes from consuming too much caffeine or being hunched over like I am right now writing this section (oops, fixed!). The fastest way to slow down the adrenaline rush is with breathing. In these situations, use the simple "four by six by six" deep breathing exercise: Inhale for four seconds, exhale for six seconds, and repeat that six times. Four seconds in, six seconds out, six times. It's only one minute of breathing, but it can change your world. Your adrenaline will go down, your sympathetic nervous system's "fight or flight" response will shut down, and your body will activate your a parasympathetic nervous system which calms you down.

FACTOR FIVE: ISOLATION

Back on that New Year's Day in 2006 I quarantined myself in a tiny apartment in a big, busy city. I thought being isolated would protect me, but it only hurt me. The isolation bred fear and worry. It made my mind race, my wheels spin, and my anxiety engine rev. It was the worst thing I could do because all I did was sit and worry about how bad things were. It's no wonder that anxiety dug in.

The solution for isolation is to extricate yourself from your solitary confinement, to push yourself out of your comfort zone and into contact with other people who can calm you down and help clear your mind. Get out of your home or work cubicle where you are stressing yourself into a storm. Get a hug, hold someone's hand, or let them put an arm around your shoulders. Seek out a therapist, perhaps one trainer in cognitive behavioral therapy (aka "talk therapy"). Touch and talk, touch and talk, those two together will always make you feel better.

Even if you don't have severe anxiety, I believe there's no downside to talking with a therapist, and that everybody should go to one. There may be things you don't think are affecting your life, when in truth, they might be a *hundred times more influential* than you believe.

The more you talk about your life with someone, the more comfortable you're going to feel as you open up. The more you open up, the more likely you are to make some big break-throughs, get better, and leave your anxiety behind. It's time for you to become Unstoppable.

Exercise: Make a Contract of Commitment

At the end of my coaching workshops each client commits to making three big changes. This is the perfect place for you to do the same. Take out piece of paper. At the top, write "I commit to the following three actions in the next 90 days:" Underneath that, state your intention to fix a health habit, to remove yourself from a certain negative environment, to take up daily gratitude journaling or thank you therapy, or whatever three action items from this book that resonated with you the most. At the bottom of the page print and sign your name, write the date, and ask a friend or family member to witness it, and perhaps even act as your accountability buddy to hold you on track to these commitments. With this in place, big breakthroughs await you on your hero's journey – starting today.

Summary

- Understand that you are on an Unstoppable Journey. Commit to the idea of kaizen – constant and never-ending improvement. You can always get better, and the best is yet to come.

- Keep yourself uncluttered. Learn to say no so that you prevent getting overwhelmed, confused, or reactive. Say yes only to what matters, plan ahead, and be as proactive as possible.

- Don't go it alone. Never allow yourself to get isolated. Keep out of your head, prevent those wheels from racing and spinning in the mud, and talk your way out of trouble when you can. There are good people out there, and they want to help you.

GIVING BACK

From the Marvel superhero movie, "Dr. Strange":

The Ancient One: "Your fear of failure is precisely what kept you from greatness. Arrogance and fear still keep you from learning the simplest and most significant lesson of all."

Dr. Strange: "Which is?"

The Ancient One: **"It's not about you. You have the choice to serve something greater than yourself."**

Dr. Strange: "I'm not ready."

The Ancient One: "No one ever is. We don't get to choose our time. Death is what gives life meaning. To know your days are numbered, your time is short."

As I finished this book, my twelve-year old pup, Bally, took a turn for the worse. It seemed like he had aged fifteen years in the last four weeks. He'd lost so much strength that he couldn't stand up on the slippery hardwood floor. I had to put my hands under his belly to aid him as he walked across the kitchen, and then I had to lift his hips as he walked over the half step in the doorway to get outside.

It was time for me to support him, just as he supported me all those years ago.

It seemed like just yesterday he was jumping on my bed, begging to sleep with "dad", or wanting to go out exploring and chasing rabbits for hours a day. Now he didn't move, didn't bark, and was barely eating. I didn't know what to do, and it was the not knowing that drove me mad. How much pain was he in? How much longer? How do you make that awful decision?

I wanted to yell. I wanted to cry. And I did. This wasn't how this book was supposed to end, but everything must, and so we went outside one last time, and he sat down in the backyard and surveyed his kingdom. It was where he had barked and sniffed as a young strong dog, and where he spent hours lying in the fresh cut grass. He put his nose up one more time chasing a scent, and I caught a glimpse of that old dog wanting to get up and run. But he couldn't. And so he looked at me and I knew he was ready to go.

It was harder than I thought it would be, ten times harder. You see, it's not just the dog, it's everything you had wrapped up in and connected to and invested in the dog. The last twelve years of my life, from the anxiety attacks all the way to this book about overcoming anxiety attacks, and everything I had done in between, and maybe more importantly, everything I hadn't done. The promise. The growth. The failures. The evolution.

A dog does so much for you, and this little guy had changed the world for me. He came into my life at my lowest point and proceeded to turn my world around. He taught me to love unconditionally, to have more energy and enthusiasm for life, to welcome people with open arms, to get out of my head and give, and to be happy being me.

It sounds so silly to say, but I was so proud of that dog, of his ability to lick an almond butter jar spotless with his long tongue, of how he entered a room so excited, whipping his tail so violently it knocked everything down in its path, of how he chased deer through the fields without a hope in hell of catching them, but with this insane belief that he could. I loved his stinky breath and his goofy, slightly embarrassed look when he squatted to poop on the neighbor's lawn—as if he knew he was caught in the act. I loved our morning ritual of having him climb on my stomach and lay his head on my chest, one that we started when he was puppy and kept going until just a few months ago. All of these things brought me joy, and got me out of my own head, reducing my anxiety, making me grateful, and giving me a greater perspective on life. He was every lesson in this book packaged up into a giant ball of fur.

Bally the Dog. The dog who never played fetch. The dog who gave every ounce of love he had. The dog who showed me how to live. The dog who showed me how to give. The one, the only, Bally the Dog. You were just what I needed.

But life goes on. Epictetus, the Stoic philosopher, said this to help us cope, *"Suppose that our servant breaks a cup. We are likely to get angry and have our tranquility disrupted by the incident. One way to avert this anger is to think about how we would feel if the incident had happened to someone else instead. If we were at someone's house and his servant broke a cup, we would be unlikely to get angry; indeed, we might try to calm our host by saying "It's just a cup; these things happen."*

It is to say, "What would you say to a friend going through the same struggle? With your outside eyes, what advice would you give? Take then, that advice and apply it to you."

Life goes on. New puppies are born. Children get a day older. Sales must be made. Books have to be written. It doesn't mean I'm not writing this with a heavy heart, but I also realize that many people are going through much worse than I am right now, and they are persisting and never quitting as they travel on their own hero's journey. This knowledge, and the Stoic perspective doesn't make me grieve less, but it reminds me to get outside of my own head and that a big part of healing – from anxiety, from loss – is to do things that matter to others. That's why I appreciate the opportunity to pour my energy into you and helping you overcome your struggles.

A few days before our final trip to the vet, a client asked, *"Craig, do you ever feel like when something goes wrong your mood changes and it's really hard to get out of it?"*

Of course, we've all had that struggle. It was very bad when my anxiety was at its worst. My wheels would spin, my mind would race, and minor problems would turn into major matters that would practically paralyze my decision-making. But no more. Today, when challenged, I am guided my personal motto, the mantra of this book, and the one line above all that you must take away:

Action Beats Anxiety. Motion Beats Meditation. Work Beats Worry.

We all have rough days. We all go through tough times. Bad things happen to good people. It's inevitable.

But what I've realized, thanks to Bally, is that the best way out of trouble is to give, to get out of your own head, to look past your own troubles, and to focus on solving other people's problems.

It's not about you. When you finally get that, when you understand that life is not about you and the money you make, the cars you drive, or the home you live in, and realize that it's only about the people you help, the service you give, and lives you transform, then everything – and I mean everything – about your perspective in life changes for the better.

When you are anxious and overwhelmed, two pathways lie before you. You can get caught up in your own head, letting your wheels spin and your anxiety engine rev, or you can direct your energy outward. You can feel bad, get overwhelmed, let life get chaotic, and allow anxiety and tension to build up inside. Or you can use the exercises in this book to get aligned with your core values, to get clarity on your vision, and to structure your life and your days around what really matters. If you're struggling, which we all do, that's OK, but it's time to get back on track, one step at a time.

Not enough sales in your business? Stop worrying and go out and give value to your clients, prospects, followers, and fans. Put in place a focused plan to change things and go out there and execute.

Not feeling sure about the future? Stop stewing about and go out and train your team, get them energized, and show them how to create the best environment for your customers.

Wishing you had a fancier car because your competitor down the street just bought something new? Stop comparing yourself to others and go out and give love, energy, time, and money to a cause that really needs it.

When you are down, give.

When you struggle, give.

When you are selfish, give.

When you have doubt, go and give.

When you're anxious and thinking about something over and over again, get out of your own head and give.

Stop sitting and stewing. Get out there and start doing.

Action Beats Anxiety. Motion Beats Meditation. Work Beats Worry.

You got this. I believe in you.

ABOUT THE AUTHOR

Craig Ballantyne is known as the *World's Most Disciplined Man* by his clients, and gives them the clarity, focus, and confidence to grow their business faster while achieving better work-life balance. For over twenty years, Craig has been sought out by publications like Forbes, Maxim, Men's Health, and GQ, and his advice has transformed the lives of over seven-million people: Physically. Financially. Mentally. Emotionally. But Craig wasn't always successful, productive, or a mentor to millions. In 2006 he hit his lowest lows, suffering from crippling anxiety attacks that sent him to the Emergency Room twice. That's when he began building the systems that he could turn his world around ... and now he is sharing his life-changing secrets with you, too.